TRUMP

VS.

CLINTON

TABLE OF CONTENTS

INTRODUCTION

Chapter 1

The United States presidential election last year was the 58th ceremonial American presidential election, held on November 8, 2016. Math tells us that, when the voters reach election day, the campaign period was 597 days old. Mothers who are expecting a newborn when Ted Cruz announced his candidacy would be sporting a toddler at this time. It was a 20month relentless race to the top, months filled with ads, polls, debates and speeches. Not to mention the left and right issues that are thrown at the candidates. The 2016 Presidential election is truly one for the books, the number of controversies, and drama is like nothing that we have ever seen.

The turn of events during the final election week was as intense as it gets. The results turned out to be a surprise to many. Nonetheless, Americans remain to be hopeful about what's coming for the next four years.

Take a look back at some of the highlights of last year's Presidential campaign. We are pulling back the curtain on Trump and Clinton's respective presidential runs to uncover what actually happened behind the stage. From party loyalties to lawsuits, all the juicy stuff. All the stories you need to know about the presidential race is all here!

PRIMARY

Chapter 2

REPUBLICAN CANDIDATES

The Republican Party is one-half of the two major political party system in the U.S. they are generally referred to as the Grand Old Party or the GOP. The party is identified after republicanism, the principal value throughout the American Revolution.

The Republican Party's current philosophy is American conservatism, which contrasts with the Democrats' modern liberalism. The center beliefs of the Republican Party are focused on the idea that each person is responsible for their own place within society. The GOP believes in keeping the government should focus essentially on the state and community level, and not at a federal level.

For the 2016 Presidential Elections, the Republicans have lined up notable candidates:

John Ellis "Jeb" Bush Sr

John Ellis "Jeb" Bush Sr. was the former governer of Florida and the brother of former president George W. Bush as well as the son of president George Bush Senior.

Ben Carson

Ben Carson, a retired neurosurgeon, was born in Detroit, Michigan. Carson went to school at Yale University and went on to graduate from the University of Michigan Medical School. Carson has authored numerous books such as One Nation, Think Big, The Big Picture and You Have A Brain.

Carson was the youngest chief of pediatric neurosurgery in the United States when was just 33 years old.

John Kasich

Kasich sought the Republican nomination for president in 2000 and in 2016. Kasich was the former governor of Ohio and a former member of congress.

Jim Gilmore

James Stuart "Jim" Gilmore III a native Virginian was born October 6, 1949. From 1998 to 2002 he became the 68th Governor of Virginia.

He graduated from the University of Virginia in 1971 and then served as a counterintelligence agent in the U.S. Army. He served the public office as a county prosecutor, then as an Attorney General of Virginia, and later on elected as Governor of Virginia.

Gilmore was a candidate for the Republican nomination for President of the United States in the 2008 and 2016 elections.

Marco Rubio

Marco Antonio Rubio is an attorney politician born on May 28, 1971. He is a junior United States Senator from Florida and has previously served as Speaker of the Florida House of Representatives.

Rubio is a Cuban-American from Miami, with degrees from the University of Florida and the University of Miami School of Law. Back in 2000, he was elected to represent Florida's 111th district under the House of Representatives. In 2002 he was appointed as House Majority Leader. Afterward, in November 2006 he was elected as Speaker of the Florida House serving 2 years.
In 2008, Rubio began teaching at Florida International University and also establish his own law firm.

Rubio successfully ran for United States Senate in 2010. An April of 2015, he announced that he would seek higher office and run for President.

Donald Trump

Donald John Trump is an American entrepreneur born on June 14, 1946. He was born and raised in New York City and studied at Wharton School with a bachelor's degree in economics in 1968.

In 1971 he took over his family's construction and real estate company and renamed it The Trump

Organization. From 1996 to 2015 he owned Miss USA pageants and has also made cameo appearances in various series and films. He also hosted and co-produced a reality series The Apprentice.

Trump announced his candidacy for president as a Republican and quickly emerged as the front-runner for his party's nomination. His 2016 presidential campaign received unprecedented media coverage and international attention.

Additional Candidates included:
- Carly Fiorina, the former CEO of Hewlett-Packard
- Chris Christie the Governor of New Jersey
- Rand Paul the Senator from Kentucky
- Rick Santorum the former Senator from Pennsylvania
- Mike Huckabee the former governor of Arkansas
- George Pataki the former Governor of New York
- Lindsey Graham the Senator from South Carolina
- Bobby Jindal the Governor of Louisiana
- Scott Walker the Governor of Wisconsin
- Rick Perry the former governor of Texas

DEMOCRATIC CANDIDATES

The Democratic Party is the world's oldest active party, and is the other half of the two major political party in the United States, sharing its position with the Republicans.

Following its legacy back to Thomas Jefferson and James Madison's Democratic-Republican Party, now we have so-called modern-day Democratic Party which was established in 1828 by Andrew Jackson.

Today, the House Democratic assembly is formed largely of reformists and centrists, but there is still a minority of conservative Democrats present.

The party's ideology of modern liberalism that pushes equal social and economic rights. One of its goals is to implement government intervention on issues such as the country's economy. The party is after increasing social programs, aid labor unions, inexpensive college tuitions, reasonable health care and equal opportunity.

For the year 2016 National Elections, the Democratic party was able to put together distinguished names on the list:

Hillary Clinton

Hillary Clinton was born in Chicago, Illinois on October 26, 1947. As a child she lived in Park Ridge, a town in Illinois outside of Chicago. Hillary Diane Rodham Clinton was the first lady, a U.S. Senator and the former Secretary of State under President Obama from 2009 to 2013.

Hillary attended Wellesley College and graduated from Yale Law School. Subsequently, she served as a congressional legal counsel and moved to Arkansas where she married the former president Bill Clinton. She then served as a Senator from 2001 to 2009 and became the First Lady of the United States from 1993 to 2001. She ran for president in 2008 but lost the Democratic nomination to Barack Obama.

She was the Democratic Party's nominee for President of the United States in the 2016 election.

Bernie Sanders

Bernie was born and raised in the Brooklyn borough of New York on September 8, 1941. He was a graduate of University of Chicago in 1964. He settled in Vermont in 1968, and ran third-party campaigns for governor and U.S. senator in the 70s. In 1981 he won as an independent candidate for mayor of Burlington, Vermont.

In 1990 he was elected to represent the congressional district of Vermont in the U.S. House of Representatives. Bernie Sanders served as a congressman for 16 years before being elected to the U.S. Senate in 2006.

Sanders has built a reputation as a leading progressive voice on key issues such as campaign finance reform, corporate welfare, global warming, LGBT rights, parental leave, and universal healthcare.

Sanders announced his campaign for the Democratic presidential nomination on April 30, 2015.

Martin O'Malley

Martin Joseph O'Malley is an American politician born on January 18, 1963. He was the 61st Governor of Maryland from 2007 to 2015. Earlier he served as a city councilor for Baltimore from 1991 to 1999 and then later on elected as Mayor and stayed in office from 1999 to 2007

From 2011 to 2013 he was a chair of the Democratic Governors Association while being a governor of Maryland. He left public office in early 2015 and acted as a visiting professor at Johns Hopkins University's Carey Business

School.

As governor, O'Malley is a known supporter of illegal immigrants and same-sex marriage in Maryland.

After seeking the Democratic Party nomination, he publicly announced his candidacy in the 2016 presidential election on May 30, 2015.

GREEN PARTY

The Green Party of the United States is a progressive political party operating inside the United States. They are often described as the eco-socialist party and is generally seen as the left-wing on the political spectrum.

Jill Stein was the Green Party candidate for the 2016 Presidential election. She received slightly more than 1% of the United States popular vote and collected none of the Electoral vote.

After the election was over Jill Stein did try and force a recount in the state of Wisconsin. Stein was not a contender but the election between Trump and Clinton in Wisconsin was too close to call. The recall would mean nothing to Stein, but with Trump declared the winner ion Wisconsin, the only person a recall could help would be Hillary. Stein also pushed for a recall in Michigan and Pennsylvania. Again Stein was not a contender but, perhaps was asking for a recount to try and help Hillary.

The Green political party is the country's fourth-largest party by the membership. The GPUS firmly believes and stands on Four Pillars, namely Ecological Wisdom, Social and Economic Justice, Grassroots Democracy, and Nonviolence and Peace. In general, it's members embrace environmentalism, non-hierarchical participatory democracy, social justice, and respect for diversity, peace, and nonviolence.

In its early years, the party was referred to as "Association of State Green Parties" until 2001 they decided to establish it as

"The Green Party United States", the party is largely composed of autonomous state or local based political entities with a weak national leadership structure that largely served to coordinate electoral activities.

During the 2000 presidential election, the party gained the public's attention when they won 2.7% vote with Ralph Nader and Winona LaDuke as their ticket. Nader was able to raised millions of dollars, which mobilized the leftist and seized national headlines with his anti-corporate campaign message. In return, he was accused of siphoning important votes away from Al Gore's campaign which then paved the way for George Bush's win for the presidency. Despite this, the party currently holds no federal or state-wide elected positions. Numerous Greens party members in the United States have positions such as the city mayors or town council members.

In 2016, the Green Party of the United States fought for equal access to the party's message for the American public to an increased coverage in the mainstream media and inclusion in the Presidential debates. The party also managed to tap 50% of independent Americans who are neither registered Democrats nor Republicans.

The party was impressed by Bernie Sander's performance and in April 2016 they aimed for Bernie Sanders and his supporters with the intention of exploring some of his ways and ideology and incorporating it within the Green Party of the United States.

LIBERTARIAN PARTY

Founded in 1971, the Libertarian Party is one of the longest serving and largest third parties of America.

Libertarians seek a middle ground between the liberal values and the conservative ones. The party strongly believes in total individual liberty and stands for pro-drug legalization, pro-choice, pro-gay marriage, pro-gun rights. The Libertarians are also for anti-government regulation of business, anti-minimum wage, anti-income tax, and pro-free trade. Generally, the Libertarians are after total economic freedom.

The Libertarian Party's (LP) general ideology revolves around the phrase "more freedom, less government and lower taxes" which is based on the traditional laissez-faire ("Hands off") philosophy.

For Years, the party has been divided between two aggressive factions, the purist libertarian group, and the moderate reform faction. The reform faction focuses mainly on popular issues such as drug decriminalization, gun rights and tax cuts as a way to attract a large number of voters. On the other hand, the devoted purist group is made up of strong anarchistic-libertarians who's advocacy is based on the principles of Ayn Rand. The purist and their allies faction firmly held control of the party from the late-1980s until the moderates took over and seized control at the 2006 national convention and completely change the party's original platform.

Currently, there are over 400 LP members holding various low-level government positions. In any given election year, the LP has since increased its nomination for the local and federal candidates more than any other US third party. However, since 1996 the Greens has shown an increase in the number of members and have maintained its following and garnering more and more media attention through the years.

CLINTON'S SUPERDELEGATES

United State's secretary of state and former first lady had a definite route towards the democratic party's presidential nomination. She's flowing in cash, running an efficient campaign team and facing just one rival, which is Senator Bernie Sanders.

The 2016 election should be easy compared to her last presidential run in 2008 when she went head to head with the historic candidacy of Barack Obama.

Bernie Sanders the primary challenger to Hillary Clinton did not make it easy for Hillary, in fact, Clinton struggled. At the New Hampshire primary, Sanders struck Clinton and got 151,000 votes compared to the 95,000 votes Clinton had. In other words, the woman widely recognized to be the Democrats' only possible presidential nominee just lost more than 60 percent of the vote to an outsider.

A political analyst said that there were two main reasons for Clinton's defeat. One is that New Hampshire has far fewer minority voters compared to other states, making it favorable for Sanders, who gets most of his support from the white people. It turns out that this was not just a New Hampshire issue. Several other states that did not have big cities with lots of minority voters decided to vote for Sanders. For example Colorado, Utah, Wyoming, Montana, Minnesota, Indiana, Alaska and Maine were all states that Bernie Sanders won in the primary. Critics also pointed out that voters did not trust Clinton, and with Sanders' undeniable authenticity, the obvious choice would be the latter. In a conducted survey entitled "honesty and trustworthiness" among voters, Sanders led 92-6.

A week before the New Hampshire primary the campaign in Iowa was very close. Clinton had a razor-thin advantage over Sanders in Iowa. Nationally Senator Bernie Sanders has a dominant 56-42 percent lead.

Despite Sanders' lead and the 56,000 more vote Sanders received, Sanders actually ended up losing the Iowa caucus. This is because of the Democrats' complex nomination process, which many of his supporters claimed to be in favor of Clinton. Under this scheme, Sanders' big national lead is completely irrelevant.

The real battle between Clinton and Sanders was the fight for "delegates", who are assigned to them state-by-state. While some states award their delegates proportionally, based on each candidate's percentage of the vote, others simply grant all their delegates to whoever finishes first. The results of the Iowa caucus gave Clinton 23 delegates to Sanders 21 delegates.

In addition to these delegates, there is also a total of 712 so-called "superdelegates." These superdelegates are party leaders and chosen officials who supports whomever they like and ignore the voters. Amid the campaign, Clinton had around 90 percent of them in her corner.

The effect? Even after Iowa and New Hampshire, Clinton defeats Sanders in the one count that actually matters, with 90 percent of the delegates.

Earned Delegates
Clinton: 32
Sanders: 36

Super Delegates
Clinton: 362
Sanders: 8

Total Delegates
Clinton: 394
Sanders: 44

It is believed that Super delegates were made to give the people who controlled the party a huge say as to who the parties candidate will be. In this case due to the large amount of baggage and email that Clinton was carrying it make have helped Trump win the presidency. Clinton's only rival, Sanders wasn't complaining. He's looking for a repeat of

Clinton's long, tough campaign against Barack Obama, in which she also posted an early lead among super delegates, then watched many of them defect as they realized Obama was going to be the nominee anyway.

Sanders said in a CBS interview. "If we continue to do well around the country, and if super delegates whose main interest in life is to make sure that we do not have a Republican in the White House and if they understand that I am the candidate who is best suited to defeat the Republican nominee, I think they will start coming over to us." The Democratic National Committee, which oversees the party's primaries, is also undermining the importance of superdelegates. If the party supports a candidate that the people don't want then the big loser is the party. The Democratic party did not fare well in this election. They did not win the presidency, they did not win back the Senate and the did not win back the House of Representatives.

It was clear that Hillary Clinton thought it was fare for her to have 90% of all these superdelegates. The party also seemed to agree. Patrice Taylor, Director of Party Affairs and Delegate Selection said, "Ultimately, each state's delegation is comprised of a diverse group of citizens like you and the Democratic leaders you have elected. This is a shameful policy where the leaders of the party think that what they think should be more important that what the voters think. The Republicans are not innocent in this behavior either. Both parties are wrong about this.

Regardless of how we look like at it, it is clear that Hillary Clinton already had a huge head start before anyone took notice. Clearly, the Clintons still had some control over the Democratic party apparatus. They used this control to influence to secure as many of the superdelegates as possible.

Hillary Clinton and Bernie Sanders were both fighting to try and reach a total of 2,383 delegates, which could be made up of primary delegates or superdelegates, to win the party's nomination.

In Democratic Primary, Clinton won 2,842 presidential primary delegates compared to Sanders 1,865 delegates. Of the 2,842 delegates Clinton received 571 superdelegates compared to sanders 45 superdelegates. If superdelegates had voted the opposite way (571 for Sanders and 45 for Clinton) then Sanders would have had 2391 and he would have won the Democratic nomination. This shows that the superdelegates was a large enough factor to decide this election.

COLORADO'S CONVENTION

The Republican part in Colorado has district and state conventions that tripped up Donald Trump. Cruz was able to navigate the primary election process to win 33 delegates to Trumps 1 delegate in Colorado.

Trump and many people were upset because it seems like state party rules were used to win the election. Clearly Cruz understood the rules and used them to his advantage. This turned out to be an important lesson for Trump. Trump realized that the election is won based on who has the most delegates. Nothing else matters. In the general election Trump and his election team concentrated on this fact.

The rules of the state were in fact changed in 2012, but this was not the reason for Trump's loss in Colorado. The rules only eliminated the meaningless straw polls that were performed.

However The Colorado Convention is not a simple process. Thousands of people descend on an stadium in Colorado Springs and then over 500 people will speak for about 20 seconds each. These people were trying to be chosen as one of one of the 37 Republican delegates. Some of the delegates are like Democratic superdelegates are selected before the process is open for the common convention voter.

The fascinating and backward way that Colorado selects their delegates has been going on for over 150 years. The election process in Colorado will probably be on the agenda of the new Republican party chairperson Ronna Romney McDaniel the niece of 2012 republican candidate: Mitt Romney.

SANDERS' FIGHT AGAINST CLINTON

Former Secretary of State Hillary Clinton's chief competitor for the nomination was Bernie Sanders. For months, Sanders and Clinton were often feisty rivals, as she progressed towards the Democratic nomination. Sanders continued to inspire a movement of millennials and had the Democratic party supported him at all then he might have been the president.

Sanders, the Vermont senator, went on to host several speeches, talking about key issues, such as universal healthcare, free higher education, and increasing the federal minimum wage. The camp of Bernie Sanders' actively directed its campaign over social media, the same platform which allowed candidate Sanders to fundraise around $200 million via small donations.

One of Sander's main advocacy and intention was to influence and encourage everybody to go to the polls and vote. Even after Clinton was declared the nominee base on the number of delegates and superdelegates she had collected, Bernie Sanders refused to concede.

And although Clinton has a clear lead on superdelegates, the Vermont senator said in an interview that he will compete for the position of

Democratic nominee until the very last primary in Washington DC. His words were "We are going to fight hard to win the primary in Washington, DC."

The superdelegates really hurt Bernie Sander's campaign. However, during this time, there were news reports that superdelegates, in reality, were not really committed as they claimed to be. Superdelegates can switch their votes at the convention or at any time before the convention. So it is correct to state that, superdelegate votes are not really Hillary's votes or Bernie's votes until votes until they are cast at the Democratic Convention.

Clinton's rival showed no sign of giving up as he sent out campaign emails to supporters and encourage them to vote and volunteer in anticipation of the final democratic primary held last June in Washington DC.

Senator Sanders was even labeled as sexist, to which he responded, "I don't think it is sexist, our focus right now is running and winning right here in California and the second point that I have made is that it is absolutely imperative that we defeat Donald Trump as a candidate for president of the United States. I believe that I am the stronger candidate."

He believed that beating Trump wasn't enough. In

one of his interview, he mentioned "We've got to work tirelessly to make sure that Trump is not president but that is not good enough," he said. The Vermont senator said in a Democratic Party "political campaigns come and go, but political and social revolutions continue."

Even towards the end of the campaign period he showed no sign of wavering and told his supporters "we take our fight for social, economic, racial and environmental justice to Philadelphia," where the Democratic convention will take place. Indeed, even after Sander's national lead of 55,000 more votes against Clinton. At the final primary election on June 14, Clinton turned into the assumptive Democratic nominee.

Naturally, Senator Sanders' supporters were not thrilled. They blamed the superdelegates nomination effect and the democratic party's way and the process of nomination. Two petitions were made by a progressive activist group, demanding that superdelegates should follow the will of the voters, which had 322,000 signatures.

"This process is undemocratic and fundamentally unfair to Democratic primary voters," said Ilya Sheyman, the advocate group's executive director. Further Sheyman said, "Democracy only works when the votes of the people not the decision of a small number of elites, are what determines the outcome of elections" she also asserted, "Super delegates must stand with voters and honor the outcomes of primaries and caucuses held across the country. The party's base simply will not tolerate any anti-democratic efforts by super delegates to thwart the will of the people."

In spite of the fact that Sanders did not authoritatively endorse Clinton he promised to work with Hillary Clinton to beat Donald Trump

On July 22, 2016, emails exchanges coming from the Democratic National Committee, Debbie Wasserman Schultz, Luis Miranda and other high position Democrat party members that seems to be working directly against Sanders in an attempt to belittle and undermine his candidacy. Debbie Wasserman Schultz, resigned just prior to the Democratic Conversion on July 24th 2016. Schultz was succeeded by Donna Brazile, another Clinton loyalist who was additionally involved in the leaks and apologized to Sanders and his supporters.

THE OUTSIDERS

The primary post-debate poll of Iowa Republicans showed the rise of the outsiders. Notable candidates who assumed that voters would be influenced by their impressive record in public office were somewhat disappointed with the poll results.

It was evident that over 60% of the people from Iowa favored either one of the four political outsiders. According to the results, Cruz received 27.64%, Trump got 24.3%, Carson was able to secure 9.3%, and Fiorina received 1.9% in votes.

Cruz, positioned himself as an outsider from the U.S. Senate that believed deeply in his faith and the constitution of the United States.

Trump, for one, sets himself as a "developer" a sharp negotiator who takes care of business, whatever it might be, and who takes pleasure in pounding the "underdogs" of today's political class.

Carson brings to the table a mix of brilliance and calm quietude, whose accomplishments as a world-class specialist are genuinely impressive. His positivity rating of 79% among Iowa assembly voters did not come as a surprise.

With Fiorina, you got the expertise of a CEO of a Fortune 500 company executive rather than a profession lawmaker.

THE DEBATES

Ever since the 1960 Presidential election debate that involved Richard Nixon and John F. Kennedy, historians had acknowledged that a televised debate had a profound effect on election results. The interest towards debates was increasingly valued.

The debates will not only help voters understand and hear the candidates address key issues prior elections, but they will also have a clear knowledge of who they want to support in the running. All thanks to the beauty of a Democratic type of government.

Here is what transpired during the 3 Presidential debates.
First Presidential Debate

First Presidential Debate
Donald Trump's self-ruling method has gone out of control in the first presidential debate as he was constrained on the defensive during the encounter with Hillary Clinton.

Instigated by moderator Lester Holt and hounded by Clinton, the Republican nominee angrily defended his record against attacks of racism, sexism and tax evasion for much of the debate held at Hofstra University, just outside New York.

Trump was able to call out Clinton on issues such as trade and her political record. These issues usually helped Trump draw level in the polls but never to a commanding lead. This move made the businessman looked under-prepared and thin-skinned as he choked his way through the debate. "It's all words, it's all sound bites," he answered after a one-sided exchange, stating that Hillary Clinton was a "typical politician: all talk, no action".

But the Democratic nominee was quick to rebut on Trump's nomadic responses and the seemingly lack of focus on the on-going debate meeting. Clinton said, "Words matter when you run for president, and they really do matter when you are president," Then went on to say, "I think Donald just criticized me for preparing for this debate. And yes I did. You know what else I did? I prepared to be president," There was a moment where Clinton attacked Trump for racism because he questioned Barack Obama's citizenship. Hillary added, "He has a long record of engaging in racist behavior. And the birther lie was a very hurtful one." Clinton also attempted to implicate that Trump was, "stiffing thousands" of contractors by declaring bankruptcy during a point in his career as a businessman. In a closing argument, Clinton pointed out Trump's record of sexism, and added that Trump had refered to women as pigs and slobs. Further see asserted that in one case, called he insulted a beauty contestant by calling her "Miss Housekeeping".

Trump then attacked Clinton's capability as president in simple terms. He said, "She doesn't have the look and she doesn't have the stamina," he said. "I've been all over the place. You decided to stay home," he added.

Clinton responded by stating her accomplishment of visiting 112 countries in her 4-year term as the secretary of state. Clinton also fired back saying "When Donald Trump spends 11 hours testifying in front of a congressional committee, he can talk to me about stamina."

This backfire against Trump and worked in favor of Clinton. The questions of stamina and temperament were a testament that Trump indeed lack focus and concentration during the uninterrupted debate, which was his first one-on-one appearance on a political debate stage.

Immediately after the debate, Trump took to the media spin room to defend his performance. Boris Epsheteyn, Trump's campaign spokesman, blamed the moderator, saying "Lester Holt interrupted Mr. Trump more. He followed up with Mr. Trump more. He was much harder on Mr. Trump."

Meanwhile, Clinton's campaign team declared that

the debate had highlighted that Trump was both "unhinged and unfit to be president" – but at the same time, they were cautious to sustain expectations.

In an interview, John Podesta, the Clinton campaign chairman, said, "He came in unprepared and what we saw was kind of a meltdown."

Clinton's campaign manager Robby Mook, cannot let the debate pass without commenting, so this is what he had to say "We'll have to see how the voters judge this." He added, "But I think the consensus of this entire debate was that Secretary Clinton was the only one on that stage prepared to be president, and I think the totality of the debate proved how deeply unfit he was."

Before the debate, Clinton spent the afternoon preparing with her campaign aides at Garden City Hotel. Meanwhile, Trump attended and participated in a pre-debate walk-through at Hofstra University.

Afterward, while Trump was taped hastily escaping in his car, Clinton told supporters at a debate watch party to keep supporting, telling them: "You saw tonight how high the stakes are."

Early on in the debate, Trump said to Clinton "Is that OK? I want you to be happy. It's very important to me," He appeared to be trying to keep everything under control and not be aggressive.

It was noticeable that during the debate Trump was sniffing heavily and was having a nasal congestion problem. He quickly grew agitated, and he repeatedly interrupted Clinton.

Trump went after Clinton's support of her husband, Bill Clinton because when Bill was preseident he has signed into law the North America Free Trade Agreement (NAFTA) in the 1990s. Trump thought it was a bad deal for American workers. The effects of NAFTA, after it was signed into law by Bill Clinton, were the loss of 700,000 American jobs that moved to Mexico. NAFTA also helped Employeers by putting more pressure on American workers to accept lower pay. The Mexican agricultural worker was also displaced which resulted in more illegal immigrants in the United states. NAFTA was also the framework which helped drive additional agreements which would help give China access to the US markets by allowing big american corporations access to invest in China.

Clinton immediately hit Trump, because of the $14 million that he got from his father through a series of loans. His father Fred Trump, a successful real estate developer helped fund the younger Trump's effort to remodel the Grand Hyatt hotel in

Manhattan and also helped him with his political connections. Trump was quick, and fired back "it was only a small loan." Trump was able to come back and jabbed Clinton for previously promoting the Trans-Pacific Partnership, the notable 12-nation trade pact brokered under the Obama administration. When Clinton was trying to answer that she no longer supports the agreement, Trump meddled with the phrases "Is it President Obama's fault?"

Clinton smiled and said, "Donald, I know you live in your own reality." Lester Holt, the debate's mediator was unmistakably experiencing considerable difficulties to stay on theme as the two nominees exchange points that faltered amongst their personal life. He particularly said that Trump was in reality, a test to control given his forceful impulse that did not necessarily address the question being asked.

The two nominees began exchanging fiery allegations. Clinton began with Trump's tax issues as when he was a businessman. Trump was quick to pledged to release his tax returns when the secretary of state released the 33,000 emails deleted from her private home server.

Clinton fired back and continued to press all the hypothetical reasons why Trump was not releasing his tax returns. Clinton stated "perhaps Trump was not as rich as he says he is, not as charitable as he says he is" and the former first lady even implied that the businessman turned politician did not pay taxes for years. Trump responded "that makes me smart" and Clinton continued, "I think he is probably not all that enthusiastic about having the rest of the country see because it must be something really important, even terrible that he is trying to hide."

While it is certainly true that Trump may not have paid taxes in years, this was due to him suffering nearly a billion dollar loss many years ago. The IRS allows losses to be written off against gains. In some sense Clinton's argument was silly because was Clinton suggesting that Trump should pay more tax then he was legally required to pay? Nobody does. If people want to give more they don't give to the United States government. They give to a charity of their choice.

After the debate, Jason Miller, Trump's senior communications adviser, avoided interrogations from reporters on whether the Republican nominee has settled his income taxes, Miller's reaction was "of course he pays taxes" and insisted that "he has paid taxes at every level."

Trump was also put on the hot seat for his past support of the Iraq war by both Clinton and the debate moderator. The Republican nominee stood by his claim that he did not support the war.

On climate change, Trump denied Clinton's claim that, "Donald thinks climate change is a hoax by the Chinese." The Republican nominee was quick to answer and said "I did not say that," however, there was an evidence of Trump's tweet in November 2012 that read, "The concept of global warming was created by and for the Chinese in order to make US manufacturing non-competitive." And there were a couple of interviews where he clearly and repeatedly refers to global warming as "a hoax". Global warming to this day is not proven. Climate Change is real, but what causes the climate change is not known. The difference between Global Warming and Climate change is that Global Warming refers to the warming of the earth as being caused by humans, while climate change is the natural change in earth temperature over the years. For example between 1100 AD and 1200 AD the world temperature was warmer than it was today according to an IPCC report in 1990. Further if you go back in time we know there were ice ages where the planet got very cold, then the planet warmed and the glaciers disappeared. This cycle repeat several times. Something caused the temperature changes when humans were not around. The question is what is that cause. Some scientists say Sun spot activity is the cause but there is no definitive proof. So while Climate change is real, global warming may be a "hoax".

Even with the Republican nominee's rugged

performance, where he repeatedly contradicted himself, Trump had already endured a number of controversies. On the night of the first debate, he didn't change his approach.

After the first Presidential debate, the only thing left to ponder is how the polls will react after it has already tightened in recent days before the debate.

Second Presidential Debate

A shaken but challenging Republican candidate Donald Trump tried at the second debate to move past the video of him talking about touching women's genitalia. The release of this video had sent Trump's presidential campaign into a plunge.

Trump define his comments as "locker room talk," and immediately issued a dismissive apology, and when pushed by Anderson Cooper, Trump claimed he never kissed or fumbled women without their consent, and tried to change the topic as quickly as possible.

Trump accused Clinton of tainting women who've accused her husband of assault and Trump added that Clinton should be "ashamed" for even addressing his comments. In a notable remark, Trump told his rival that if he's elected, "you'd be in jail" he pledged to designate a prosecutor to investigate Clinton's email controversy.

Trump's overall performance, directing the same fury lifted his outsider bid all the way to the GOP nomination, may have been the key to subduing a large number of his supporters.

After taking the stage, both nominees said a brisk hello but bypassed the usual traditional handshake. Clinton then cut to the chase and went on with her strategy that directed at letting Trump hang himself. Clinton avoided interrupting Trump's answers, and while she had sharp words to say about her opponent's video comments — the former first lady bolsters Trump's unsuitability for office.

"This is who Donald Trump is," Clinton had this to say for his recorded comments while pointing to its consistency with insulting remarks he's made public during a campaign about Muslims, Hispanics, African-Americans, and POWs. "And the question for us, the question our country must answer is that this is not who we are." Soon after, in response to Trump nagging about her deleted emails, Clinton finally hit back with: "OK, Donald. I know you're into big diversion tonight, anything to avoid talking about your campaign and the way it's exploding and the way Republicans are leaving you."

In general for the second debate, Clinton projected a poker face, showing disinterest and occasional musing as Trump continued on the attack. And at one point Trump had nothing to say but "Believe me, she has tremendous hate in her heart."

The downside of the first and second debate was that much of the time went to the conflict and counter-conflict over Trump's taped comments and the Clintons' own history. Top concerns and issues like creating more jobs were left with limited attention. However, there was a point in the debate where economic exchange was discussed and revolved around the candidate's respective tax plans.

When asked what's their take on the tax code to ensure that the wealthiest Americans pay their share, Trump responded first by discussing the capital gains treatment of carried interest is to blame, and he'd eliminate this saying. "One of the greatest provisions for people like me, to be honest with you," The Republican pledge for tax cuts for corporations of all sizes and a "big league" cut for the middle class. Being true to his character he warned Clinton saying "raise your taxes really high." and use this argument and press that Clinton represents the status quo and that she accomplishing nothing over her 30 years in public service.

Clinton answered by dismissing Trump's answer in its totality as untrue following a statement "I'm sorry I have to keep saying this, but he lives in an alternative reality."

Clinton stated, seeing the irony of quarreling over the code with a nominee who has refrained from paying his income tax for about two decades.

She went on to call Trump's plan a gift to the rich, "more than the Bush tax cuts by at least a factor of two." On the other hand, she said she'd offer a tax shield to anybody acquiring under $250,000 from any hikes while pushing the Buffett Rule for anybody gaining over $1 million and an additional charge on revenues above $5 million.

This exchange gave a chance for the moderators to follow up with Trump about his alleged nonpayment. And he appeared to acknowledge it. When asked if he used the $916 million loss he recorded in 1996 to offset paying income taxes in subsequent years. Trump confirmed this. As a fact check it is legal to do this and anyone with loss in the stock market, real estate or other areas of investment is allowed to do this. The IRS does limit how much one can recover per year. So Trump would only be able to recover a small portion of his loss each year. Trump also stated that the same write off was taken by Clinton's top donors.

The repeated dismal encounter at least ended on a lighter note. Prompted by the last audience questioner asking to name something admirable about the opposition, Clinton referred to Trump's children as wealth to him while Trump admired Clinton's determination. For a moment in the debate, it felt like a genuine yet careful exchange of goodwill. The Second Presidential debate then concluded by a handshake.

Third Presidential Debate

The third Presidential debate happened in Vegas, and this time what happened in Vegas won't stay in Vegas. Hillary Clinton and Donald Trump took part in their final TV debate before November's presidential election.

It was the last chance for Hilary Clinton and Donald Trump to take advantage of a national stage and make some impressive moments and statements for the voters.

Prior to the third Debate Donald Trump meet with several women who had accused Bill Clinton, Hillary's husband, of rape at a press conference. The women included Paula Jones, Kathleen Wiley and Juanita Broaddrick as well as others. Kathy Shelton, a women had been raped many years ago. Hillary Clinton was the lawyer who defended the accused rapist and got her client off as not guilty and then laughed about it. Trump supported these women to show that he did care about women and because it showed that Hillary had been an enabler for Bill Clinton's womanizing ways for decades.

The Republican nominee's performance in the first two debates came with a blow. Allegations of sexual assault led to a steep drop in Trump's state polls.

Trump displayed political progress and decided to invite Pat Smith, a Benghazi victim's mother, and Malik Obama, Barack's estranged half-brother. He also mentioned in a repeated instance that elections will be rigged.

Clinton started the final debate with a clear lead but had to keep her head above water because of WikiLeaks's release of John Podesta's hacked emails. Podesta was the chairman of Hilary Clinton's presidential election campaign. Analysts said that the third debate could be the answer to resolving her credibility issues. It was also a missed opportunity for the Democratic nominee to offer herself as a viable option to Republicans who have been jumping off Trump's bandwagon and to maybe expand the Democratic map and enter red states like Arizona and Georgia.

Fox News' Chris Wallace was the chosen moderator for the final debate, this is the first time an anchor from the network has been selected to oversee a general election debate. Wallace was expected to be tough and unforgiving to both nominees. Wallace prepared six 15-minute segments, these segment included topics of immigration, debt and entitlements, Supreme Court, the economy, foreign hot spots, and most importantly eligibility to be president.

On the first debate segment, one of Wallace's topic was late-term abortions, Trump used this instance to accuse Clinton of supporting a practice in which "in the ninth month you can ... rip the baby out of the womb of the mother just prior to the birth of the baby."

Trump has made it clear from the start of his campaign that he abhors immigrants, saying: "They're bringing drugs. They're bringing crime. They're rapists." From more than a year into his campaign, Trump has not changed his stand on the issue, doubling down on the assumption that immigrants are criminals during the debate.

During the debate, Clinton got the chance to address the WikiLeaks hack by questioning Trump's active support of Russian espionage against "the American people." Which Trump replied, "Now we can talk about Putin. I don't know Putin. He said nice things about me. If we got along well, that would be good."

When Trump challenged whether the election espionage was linked to Russia, Clinton fired back and said, "He'd rather believe Vladimir Putin than the military and civilian intelligence professionals who are sworn to protect us." Trump answered, "She doesn't like Putin because Putin has outsmarted her at every step of the way." Again, Trump emphasized that Putin "is not my best friend." And added, "But if the United States got along with Russia, it wouldn't be so bad."

The debate moderator, Wallace brought up Trump's pessimist cries about what he describe as a rigged election. Wallace stated that Kellyanne Conway, Trump's campaign manager, Trump's running mate, and Trump's daughter have agreed to recognize the poll results. To which Trump's answer was "I will tell you at the time, but I will keep you in suspense." Clinton was quick to respond to Trump's remark, saying: "This is horrifying. Let's be clear about what he is saying and what that means. He is taking down our democracy." Clinton added that that statement is a remarkable admission and a direct challenge to the American democratic system suggested by a Republican nominee. This statement would come back to haunt Hillary after the election when it was she, not Trump who questioned the elections. There were riots in the streets and Hillary was trying joining a recount effort by the Green party in Wisconsin, Michigan and Pennsylvania. This was one of the big faults that been brought up during the election. Hillary had a public position on an issue, while have a different private opinion on the same issue. Here was an example where Hillary publicly stated that the American Democracy was at risk if the losing candidate did not accept the results. But when she lost, her private position of wanting to win took over.

The process of picking a running mate is often called the "veepstakes." The term suggests that the process is a game, and it is significant to make the right decision. According to history, nine vice presidents have become president due to the death or resignation of the president, but promising vice presidential candidates tend to receive less criticism than federal judges and cabinet picks.

Presidential candidates may decide on their running mates for many reasons. Some believe expand their appeal and improve their chances in the election by choosing a running mate very distinct from themselves. Others choose a running mate based on geography, to win over areas where support may be limited. And some concentrate on selecting an individual who would be a capable vice president or president.

Democratic Party Democratic vice presidential candidate Tim Kaine. A US junior senator who served as mayor of Richmond from 1998 to 2001 and a governor of Virginia from 2006 to 2010. Kaine also acted as the chair of the Democratic National Committee from 2009 to 2011.

Three days before the start of the Republican National Convention, Republican presidential nominee Donald Trump announced on social media that he had selected Indiana Gov. Mike Pence as his running mate. And on July 16, 2016, Trump formally introduce Pence as his "partner" in the race at a news conference in New York City.

Pence, at age 57, is the governor of Indiana. He describes himself as "a Christian, a conservative, and a Republican, in that order." Pence earlier served in the United States House of Representatives representing Indiana's 2nd Congressional District from 2001 to 2013.

A vice presidential debate took place on October 4, 2016, at Longwood University in Farmville, Virginia. It was considered to be the only vice presidential debate of the 2016 general election season.

Participants in the vice presidential debate included Tim Kaine and Mike Pence.

The Commission on Presidential Debates is a nonpartisan organization who takes charge and oversees the general election debates. The commission announced that Libertarian vice presidential nominee Bill Weld, and Green Party vice presidential nominee Ajamu Baraka, were not invited to attend the debate. The CPD required the nominee to have a 15 percent or higher polling average in order to be invited to the debate. During the time, the Libertarian Party bet was polling at 8.4 percent in the polls used by the CPD. And the Green Party's Baraka registered only a 3.2 percent rating. The two failed to satisfy the CPD's criteria for inclusion. The commission is left with a Kaine versus Pence match.

Wisconsin Gov. Scott Walker helped Pence prepare by playing the role of Kaine on mock debate sessions. On the Democratic side, D.C. attorney Bob Barnett played the role of Pence during Kaine's mock debate sessions. Barnett also helped Clinton with debate prep in the 2016 Democratic primaries by playing as Vermont Sen. Bernie Sanders.

Both candidates, Indiana Governor Mike Pence and Virginia Senator Tim Kaine, spent most of the debate talking about Trump and Clinton the two main candidates for president. They also attacked the policy proposals of the rival's campaign.

The rules of the debate allowed Pence and Kaine to talk to one another during the 90-minute-long event. But this lead to a mush up, the two often talked at the same time or interrupt while the other was speaking.

Pence criticized Clinton's policies during her time as secretary of state for the current situation in the Middle East. He said her policies only allowed the

Islamic State group to grow in strength and double in numbers. Pence also called Clinton over what he called a "newly emboldened Russia."

Kaine, on the other hand, stated that the Republican's Trump cares about himself before anyone else. And he challenged Pence and claimed that Trump had business connections with Russia that he "refuses to disclose."

Both vice presidential candidates agree that action should be taken to protect civilians in northern Syria. Pence suggested the creation of a no-fly zone in the area. He said that if Russia is connected to the attacks on the Syrian city of Aleppo, then the United States forces should attack Syrian military targets. The two men also settled on the issue of the increasing need for criminal justice reforms.

During the debate, Pence praise Trump's character as a businessman who operated many successful businesses and has created thousands of jobs. Kaine however, was quick to counter by repeatedly demanded that Trump releases his tax records. Many Democrats believe that the business mogul has not paid federal taxes for years.

On the issue of tax cuts, Kaine said Trump's plan to cut taxes would only help rich people and eventually lead to a recession. Pence was firm and said that Clinton's economic plan would clearly increase taxes and government spending.

Kaine also scrutinized Trump for his stand that more countries should have nuclear weapons. Pence claimed that more nuclear weapons would make us safer.

When the debate was done, political analyst said they were pleased that the both the vice presidential candidate talked generally about politics, and not of personal nature.

John Hudak said, "It stands in contrast to the first presidential debate, which was very personally oriented, very focused on scandals, very focused on guttural politics, and not so much about what the future of America is going to look like."

Lisa Spies who worked for Pence when he served in the U.S. Congress, said: "We got details, we got facts, we got numbers." Spies also noted, "During the presidential debate, we had adjectives and adverbs, and we had insults thrown at each other, and name-calling at each other. Tonight, even though there were interruptions, they were both stating what their policies would be."

Supporters of the two candidates accused the other side of running a sloppy campaign. John Podesta, the chairman of Hillary Clinton's drive for the presidency, criticized Donald Trump. Podesta in a statement said, "I think he has run an insult-driven campaign and I think that what Tim Kaine did tonight was to challenge Mike Pence to try to defend the hateful campaign."

Jeb Hensarling a known Trump supporter said, "It's clear that all the name-calling was coming from Tim Kaine. I mean, some of his charges were so over the top. It's something I would expect to see in a grocery store tabloid. I just think he lost credibility with the American people. He was just lodging charge after charge after charge."

THE SCANDALS

Hillary Clinton's Private Emails

Even with the State Department's clearing thousands of pages of Hilary's e-mail, controversy still encompasses Hillary's use of a private e-mail server over allotted departmental servers amid her time as Secretary of State. The secretary of state insisted that the issue was only used by her detractors, some are still very suspicious that Clinton may have deleted e-mails that belong in the public domain. Hillary has admitted to deleting a few e-mails that she believe was personal.

This scandal is one that numerous members of the GOP will need to use to bring doubt upon Clinton as having purposely concealed data from the American people. Whether it'll stick is completely far from being obviously true, but do not expect this issue to die soon because the matter will come up over and over until the end of the decision.

Hillary Clinton decided prior to set up a private email computer server prior to her taking the job as Secretary of State. This was against government policy. It would be illegal for her to receive or send classified documents. This is not simple thing to do. First you have buy the computer system, then you need get the system configured and finally you have to have someone maintain the server. Any private citizen is allowed to set up a private email server. The issue that one runs into is when you work for government and you deal with classified information, then when the documents and emails sit on the server which is unsecured, you are breaking the law.

Hillary did not use a standard state department email address that ended with '@state.gov,' instead she used '@ClintonEmail.com. The physical server was kept in her house in Chappaqua, New York.

Initially when Clinton started to travel as secretary of state she used a blackberry phone which was connecting to her server using an unencrypted protocol. She should have been using Encryption software on her phone to have her emails encrypted. Communication between a phone and an email server will be routed by several servers on internet. Each machine that the message passes through is called a hop. In would not be uncommon for a message to go through 20 or more hops. At each one of these hops and even in between these hops a foreign government or a hacker can copy the message that is being sent or received. When the data is encrypted the party that intercepts the message cannot read it. But if the data is unencrypted then they can read the message just like a Microsoft Word document on your computer.

On July 5th 2016, Jim Comey, the director of the FBI said that Hillary was extremely careless in her handling highly sensitive classified information. Jim Comey went on to say that no reasonable prosecutor would bring such a case. The second statement by Comey is strange since he clearly indicated that she mishandled top secret classified documents. Being ignorant is not an excuse. If you think it is then just try not paying your income taxes and property taxes and see if your assets are not seized and your house foreclosed on.

Jim Comey on July 7th 2016 appeared before congress and was questioned by Trey Gowdy (Republican from South Carolina). Below is a transcript that shows that Hill

Gowdy asked, "Secretary Clinton Stated that she never received classified email over her private server. Is that true?"

Comey responded, "Our Investigation found that there was classified information sent."

Gowdy asked, "Secretary Clinton said there was not marked classified on her emails either sent or received. Was that true?"

Comey responded, "That is not true. There were a small number of portion markings on I think 3 of the documents."

Gowdy asked, "Secretary Clinton said I did not send any classified material to anyone on my email. There is no classified material. Was that true?"

Comey replied, "No there was classified material emailed."

Gowdy continued with, "Secretary Clinton said she used just one device. Was that true?"

Comey replied, "She used multiple devices during her 4 years as secretary of state."

Gowdy then asked, "Secretary Clinton said all work related emails were returned to the state department. Was that true?"

Comey replied, "No we found work related emails. Thousands that were not returned."

Gowdy continue with, "Secretary Clinton stated that neither she nor anyone else deleted emails from her personal account. Was that true?"

Comey answered, "That is a harder one to answer. We found traces of work related emails. On devices or in slack space. Whether they were deleted or when a server was changed out something happened to them. There is no doubt that work related emails were removed electronically from the email system."

Gowdy asked, "Secretary Clinton said her lawyers read every one of her emails and were overly inclusive. Did the lawyers read the email content individually?"

Comey quickly replied, "No"

Gowdy continued to question why Comey did not use these false exculpatory statements against Hillary Clinton and why a common soldier from the military that emailed classified pictures to himself would be discharged from the Military but Hillary Clinton would get a pass and be allowed to be elected to commander in chief.

Hillary Clinton's Benghazi Failure

On September 11th 2012 United States government facilities in Benghazi Libya were attacked by Islamic forces from a group know to the United States as Ansar al-Sharia. The result of the attack left four Americans dead, it was under Hillary Clinton's term as the Secretary of State when it happened.

Hillary told her daughter that a terrorist group was responsible for the attack, however what Hillary and the Obama administration told the public was that the attack was a spontaneous attack that was cause by a Youtube.com video:

https://www.youtube.com/watch?v=kovTkWnasYk

Hillary later tried to explain why she had two position. She claimed that the information was changing by the hour and it was complicated.

But 24 hours after the attack Hillary Clinton told Hesham Kandil, the Egyptian Prime Minister, that the Benghazi attack, "had nothing to do with the film." Clinton also stated that "it was a planned attack – not a protest."

This would seem to point to Clinton and/or the Obama administration lying about what happened. Obama at the time was worried about being re-elected. Thus news about terrorists was unacceptable since The Obama Administration was saying terrorism is on the run.

What is strange is if you have American's in serious trouble then the logical conclusion that a rational person, that does not have a secret agenda, would be to just send help. So why didn't Hillary and the Obama administration just send the military to help? They had no way of knowing how long the compound at Benghazi could hold out. Or why didn't they ask one our allies in the area to help? Or did they not really want to send help?

Why was Ambassador Stevens in Benghazi in the first place? Benghazi is not the capital of Libya. What was he doing there? Some have speculated that he was helping the Obama administration with gun running for Libyan jihadists fighting Moammar Gadhafi, the dictator of Libya. If this were the case then letting Stevens die would tie-up loose ends. Did Clinton and Obama support sending arms to terrorists in Libya and later Syria? If this were true would they ever want this to be public knowledge? Of course many simply believe that this is impossible the president would never provide guns to terrorists or people that could cause harm to Americans or other civilians. Right? Well of course the answer wrong. President Obama already did this in the United States of American when he authorized "Operation Fast and Furious." Fast and Furious was an operation that was supposed to help the United States destroy drug cartels that were doing "illegal drug business" within the United States. The operation was a complete failure. This operation ended up putting two-thousand weapons in the hands of the drug dealers so that the government could supposedly trace the guns. The weapons were used by drug lords to kill hundreds of Mexicans and a United States Border Agent. Guns From Obama's Fast and Furious program also were linked to Drug kingpin Joaquin "El Chapo" Guzman. He was found to have a .50-caliber rifle from the Fast and Furious which could be used to shoot down a helicopter. Obama and the White

House that Hillary was a part of has attempted several times to assert executive privilege to prevent Congress from seeing documents related to Fast and Furious.

So one can clearly see that the Obama administration had no trouble giving out guns to drug lords. So It is not the big a leap to believe that Hillary and Obama were giving out guns to terrorist to try to get them to take down the Libyan dictator Gadhafi. Although Gadhafi had become less of threat in his old age and had given up materials for his Nuclear and weapons of mass destruction program in 2003 and Libya had signed the Nuclear Non-Proliferation Treaty (NPT). This brings up the question of the judgment of Hillary and Obama since Gadhafi was really not a threat to the United States. Thus what we see is Hillary and Obama trying to bring about change in the Middle East, but ending up allowing Terrorism to grow in Libya, Syria, IRAQ and Yemen. While at the same time appeasing the Terrorist State IRAN by sending millions of dollars in cash and signing an agreement with IRAN that allows them to build nuclear weapons.

There were hundreds of requests for additional security from Ambassador Chris Stevens that were sent by Stevens several days before the attack on Benghazi even started. All the requests were ignored by Hillary and the State department. Why was Hillary surprised when an attack occurred on

9/11?

There are a lot of questions and no answers. This in itself speaks to trustworthiness of Hillary Clinton. She and the Obama administration were not disclosing what they were doing. And the result was the Middle East became very unstable, Leaders in Egypt, Libya, Syria, Yemen and IRAQ were either toppled or cornered. The destabilization of all these countries has cause a massive refugee problem and the rise of Al-Qaeda, a large terrorist organization that now exists in multiple countries.

Ted Cruz's Curiosity on Government Shutdown

Congressman Ted Cruz had an extensive turn in the administration shut down of 2013, making a line in the sand opposite President Obama. It was a move that angered many, incorporating legislators in his own party. Castigate for forcing the issue without having no plan to escape the shutdown, numerous GOP representatives lay the fault of the failure decisively at Cruz's feet.

While that could be subdued, Cruz kept on using an administration shut down as a strategy, totally overlooking that the last shutdown brought about wide disappointment with the Republican party. Cruz should understand that while his base may not really like the administration they have, they would prefer essentially not to see everything close down.

Carly Fiorina's Blunders as a CEO

While asserting your experience as a CEO as a positive, you'll likewise need to acknowledge the negatives, and Carly Fiorina has a noteworthy screw up on her resume - a forced resignation as CEO of Hewlett-Packard Company. This came as an immediate consequence of her driving a merger with Compaq against overwhelming restriction from half of the shareholders. Her progressions inside likewise infuriated many majority representatives.

The outcome? A decrease in stock costs that was far more honed than whatever is left of the tech world being dinged by the blasting of the tech bubble. Keeping in mind there was an increase in income, it was totally offset by the expansion owing debtors collected during her time. When she was constrained out of HP, numerous representatives cheered, and HP's stock bounced extensively, including $3 billion dollars in one day.

Sanders's Separation from the Democratic Party

For all practical purposes, Bernie Sanders is an independent. As far as the party alliance goes, he's running as a Democrat particularly for across the country vote access and to push the debate of left-wing legislative issues.

Nonetheless, among the more moderate Democrats, they may not consider Sanders to be a genuine member of the party and not a serious probability for selection. In the event that people questioning his legitimacy, he will be unable to change the debate as much as he'd like, to state nothing of an actual designation.

Ted Cruz Citizenship

To the disarray of civics students throughout, Ted Cruz was conceived in Canada, however, numerous law experts trust it won't block him from running for the administration. Be that as it may, it's the kind of story that, in the age where birthers still claim Obama is not a rightful president because of his birth issues, an issue that will not go away.

Regardless of the possibility that the legitimacy issue disappears, there's truly no getting around jokes about his birth home. Such subjects can divert from Cruz's policy claims, and turn a serious running into a gag line at the comedy bar.

TRUMP VERSUS MEGAN KELLY

The famed story of Fox News host Megyn Kelly and Republican nominee Donald Trump and created a bang during the Republican Party primaries that seemed to have died down in the past months.

The fight between Trump and Kelly started Aug. 6, 2015, at the first Republican presidential debate, when the two had a controversial back-and-forth.

In the opening round of questions, the host of The Kelly File went directly after the Republican front runner and poll leader, business billionaire Donald Trump.

In a question directed at Trump, Kelly said, "Mr. Trump, one of the things people love about you is you speak your mind and you don't use a politician's filter," she said. "However, that is not without its downsides, in particular, when it comes to women. You've called women you don't like, 'fat pigs,' 'dogs,' slobs, and disgusting animals."

Trump inserted a one-liner: "Only Rosie O'Donnell."

Kelly pushed on. "No, it wasn't," she said. "Your Twitter account has several disparaging comments about women's looks. You once told a contestant on

Celebrity Apprentice it would be a pretty picture to see her on her knees. Does that sound to you like the temperament of a man we should elect as president, and how will you answer the charge from Hillary Clinton, who was likely to be the Democratic nominee, that you are part of the war on women?"

Trump countered by claiming that "the big problem this country has is being politically correct." He added "Frankly, what I say, and oftentimes it's fun, it's kidding," he said. "We have a good time. What I say is what I say. And honestly Megyn, if you don't like it, I'm sorry."

Another question that stood out to Trump was Kelly asking him "Mr. Trump, in 1999, you said you were, quote, 'very pro-choice.' Even supporting partial-birth abortion. You favored an assault weapons ban as well. In 2004, you said in most cases you identified as a Democrat. Even in this campaign, your critics say you often sound more like a Democrat than a Republican, calling several of your opponents on the stage things like 'clowns' and 'puppets.' When did you actually become a Republican?" Trump find this question out of bounds and offensive to which he feels Kelly should issue an apology.

After the debate, Trump tweeted "Wow, @megynkelly really bombed tonight. People are going wild on twitter! Funny to watch."

Despite Clinton's lead in polls, it did not end there. Former Speaker of the House and a republican politician, Newt Gingrich tells Megyn Kelly
"I mean, do you want to go back through the tapes on your show recently?" he asked. "You are fascinated with sex, and you don't care about public policy."

Kelly asked if Trump was a "sexual predator" after mentioning a hot-mic "Access Hollywood" tape from 2005 in which Trump boasted of being able to grope women without their consent because he claimed to be famous. The Republican nominee described his comments as a "locker room banter." and nothing more.

Kelly said in an interview with Charlie Rose on October 8th, 2015 that neither she nor Fox News wanted "any sort of war" with Trump.

Kelly added "He was obviously upset. That's fine. He's running for president, it's not a fun business, there's going to be ups and downs, and I know he considered that a down," On the same interview she mentioned. "So we just wanted to forge forward and try to put it behind us, not pour any more fuel on that fire."

After the interview, Kelly made it clear that she

wouldn't engage in a strife with Trump. However, there is no stopping Trump's agenda against Kelly. This prompted the news anchor to respond to social media after a series of attacks thrown at her.

In a series of tweet exchanges, Trump tweeted "Isn't it terrible that @megynkelly used a poll not used before (I.B.D.) when I was down but refuses to use it now when I am up?"

To which Megyn Kelly replied with a picture of result polls and a tweet saying "@realDonaldTrump - Facts matter."
Kelly was able to discuss the matter with ABC News last February.

Kelly told ABC News "It was bizarre because I became the story. He was so very focused on me that I became the story, and you know, you never want to be the story when you're a news person," she said. "You want to be covering the story, so it was like an 'Alice Through the Looking Glass' experience."

In a one-on-one interview with Trump that aired last May, Kelly, said it took her a while to find the right time to reach out to Trump.

"In April there was a lull in the tweet storm, and I seized on the opportunity," Kelly added. "I had been looking for months for just the right window to go in there. But every time I thought I was there, he'd start up again, whether it was boycotting the second Fox News debate or calling me crazy and sick after the third debate."

During Kelly's the interview with Trump, the real estate mogul said he thought Kelly's question about his comments about women "was unfair" but seemed to realize her decision to ask it. He said "I don't really blame you because you're doing your thing. But from my standpoint, I don't have to like it."

The months following the interview the tension between Trump and Kelly seemed to have eased with no significant flare-ups.

Shortly after the election Megyn Kelly left the Fox Network to go to NBC.

POSITIONS

Chapter 3

CLINTON AND TRUMP POSITIONS

Clinton for higher Taxes vs. Trump for lower taxes

Clinton and Trump have very different points of view regarding taxes. Here is Hillary's position:

"I want to make sure the wealthy pay their fair share, which they have not been doing. I want the Buffett Rule to be in effect, where millionaires have to pay 30 percent tax rates instead of 10 percent to nothing in some cases. I want to make sure we rein in the excessive use of political power to feather the nest and support the super wealthy."

Here is Trump's position:

"Middle-income Americans and businesses will experience profound relief, and taxes will be greatly simplified for everyone. I mean everyone. Reducing taxes will cause new companies and new jobs to come roaring back into our country."

Clinton for Free Trade vs. Trump for Fair Trade

Americans have been presented with a diverse set of trade policies both nominees. On Clinton's side, she has rejected CAFTA and the TPP yet finds that the worldwide economy needs free trade. While Trump disputes for a more Protectionist financial approach in saying "Our nation is getting ripped off."

Worldwide trade is both a complicated and notable topic that Americans ought to consider when voting in the year's presidential election. Trump pushes for a more safe position on trade which is like Mercantilism. In layman terms, protectionism contends for a "great balance of trade" by sending out more than bringing in and ensuring domestic industries rivaling imported products by means of taxes. Trump said that he would renegotiate NAFTA and force a 35% tax on Mexican imports. With Chinese imports, Trump needs to require a 45% duty. In the first presidential debate between Clinton and Trump, Trump said "We have to renegotiate our trade deals. And, Lester, they're taking our jobs, they're giving incentives, they're doing things that, frankly, we don't do. Let me give you the example of Mexico. They have a VAT tax. We're on a different system. When we sell into Mexico, there's a tax. When they sell in -- automatic, 16 percent, approximately. When they sell into us, there's no tax. It's a defective agreement. It's been defective for a long time, many years, but the politicians haven't done anything about it."

Trump is showing here that laws or action of other countries can give them an advantage.

Thus a tax to equalize or make the trade fair or equal for both countries needs to be put in place.

Put differently; free trade can take into consideration inventive consumption to occur. Trump said "I am all for free trade, but it's got to be fair. When Ford moves their massive plants to Mexico, we get nothing." Trump is correct because the record shows there were employment issues in the manufacturing industry and NAFTA and unfair trade or manipulated trade is to blame.

Trump is vocal about supporting free trade but is also insisted that "the problem with free trade is you need really talented people to negotiate for you." One coherence with Trump is that he supposes America is being exploited. For instance, on the TPP Trump believes China is going to "come in, as they always do, through the back door and take advantage of everyone." On global exchange arrangements like NAFTA and TPP, Clinton adopts an alternate strategy. Clinton has altered her opinion on the TPP. At first, she called it, the "gold standard" of trade. Later she said, "I absorbed new info and changed my mind to oppose TPP." This kind of fluctuating on global trade strategies is something Clinton has been scrutinized for.

Clinton for Open Borders vs Trump for Closed borders

On the third presidential debate, the candidates couldn't avoid wandering off topic and not addressing the topic as flat out as the topic deserves, however, they raised some essential points and their stance on immigration turned out to be clear.

Trump began by connecting illegal immigration to the country's the drug trade. While drugs are fundamentally a U.S. Customs and Border Protection issue, there is no denying that unlawful immigration is a component of drug trafficking. Trump mentioned, that there are criminals infiltrating the United States over the U.S.- Mexican border.

His point that whether we are a nation or not, relies on upon whether we have a border or not, is essentially right. This analysis, in a manner of speaking, is correct. Trump points out that the best solution for the issue is building a divider over the southern border and have Mexico pay for it.

Unlike Trump's wall proposition, Hillary Clinton did not give solid recommendations around this issue. She doesn't agree with Trump about building a wall, in spite of the fact that there are unlawful migrants going over the borders. She did say however that all violent criminal immigrants ought to be deported. However, it is more likely that she should just turn a blind eye to illegal immigration as President Obama has done for the eight years of his presidency.

Clinton discussed a path to citizenship for the 11 million unlawful immigrants in the US, claiming that their legalization will bring them out of the shadows and along these lines make America more secure. Clinton said she would take a shot at comprehensive immigration reform within her first 100 days of her Presidency.

Donald Trump explains that all illegal migrant should be extradited from the United States. While over the span of the campaign he has mellowed his position on this issue to some degree, despite everything he holds this view. The issue for Trump on this position is a legal due process. In the United States, we have a constitutional right to due process. This applies to anybody in the country. It implies that there must be legal oversight to deporting foreigners.

More than anything, the debate exchanges just touched the surface of the elaborate issue of migration in the United States.

Clinton for ObamaCare vs Trump for Getting rid of Obamacare

At the focal point of the debate among the presidential hopefuls is President Barack Obama's 2010 health care trademark, Obamacare. Previous President Bill Clinton, spouse of Democratic presidential nominee Hillary Clinton, called the health care law "the craziest thing on the planet" then attempting to stroll back his remarks a day later.

The former president also added "So you've got this crazy system where all of a sudden 25 million more people have health care and then the people who are out there busting it, sometimes 60 hours a week, wind up with their premiums doubled and their coverage cut in half. It's the craziest thing in the world," probing the Affordable Care Act which has produced an increasing number of premiums for middle-class Americans who don't qualify for subsidies.

As a part of her health care plan, Hillary Clinton, as per MedScape, needs to amend Obamacare by expanding on the working parts of the law and widen the insurance coverage while bringing down the expenses of exchange plan premiums and high deductibles

Clinton wants an administration-run health plan or "open choice" in each state to contend with private plans in the trades and would bring down the maximum amount that a person needs to contribute toward a premium. She would likewise make an expense credit of up to $2500 per individual or $5000 per family to counterbalance out-of-pocket spending that surpasses 5 percent of wage. The Democratic nominee would likewise bring down the age that Americans can get into Medicare to 55.

She likewise tended to some Obamacare's issues amid the second presidential debate, when she was questioned regarding the increasing expenses of medical coverage premiums. To which the secretary of state replied "I'm going to fix it because I agree with you. Premiums have gotten too high. Copays, deductibles, prescription drug costs. I've laid out a series of actions that we can take to try to get those costs down,"

The Secretary of state also added, "I don't want people to forget when we're talking about reining in the costs, which has to be the highest priority of the next president when the Affordable Care Act passed, it wasn't just that 20 million got insurance who didn't have it before. But that in and of itself was a good thing. I meet these people all the time, and they tell me what a difference having that insurance meant to them and their families."

Hillary was firm on her statement about Affordable Medical Care saying "I want very much to save what works and is good about the Affordable Care Act. But we've got to get costs down. We've got to provide additional help to small businesses so that they can afford to provide health insurance. But if we repeal it, as Donald has proposed, and start over again, all of those benefits I just mentioned are lost to everybody, not just people who get their health insurance on the exchange. And then we would have to start all over again,"

Trump, on the other hand, has systematically vowed that if he is elected president, he will abolish Obamacare and replace it with free-market resolutions for uninsured or underinsured Americans.

Under Tump's plan, health insurers could sell policies across state lines. The New York City billionaire said this will open competition. People could also use pre-tax dollars to obtain coverage and individuals could open health savings accounts under Trump's plan. Open-ended federal contributions to state Medicaid programs with stop grants intended to give states more freedom in spending the money.

Trump's seven-point scheme highlighted on his website which promotes cutting waste and less expensive medication costs would likewise require value transparency from all medical services suppliers, particularly specialists and social insurance associations like centers and healing facilities. He contends that people ought to have the capacity to shop, to locate the best costs for exams or other medicinal related procedure.

What's more, the businessman turned politician is supporting for the dismissal of limits to passage into free markets for medication suppliers that offer reliable, safe, and less expensive products. Congress will require the guts to step far from the uncommon interests and make the right decision for America, he contends. He clarifies that in spite of the fact that the pharmaceutical business is in the private division, drug organizations provide a public service. Trump believes that permitting consumers access to import safe and dependable drugs from abroad will bring more alternatives.

The Republican bet is also an advocate of improving mental health plans. "Families, without the ability to get the information needed to help those who are ailing, are too often not given the tools to help their loved ones. There are promising reforms being developed in Congress that should receive bi-partisan support," as stated on his website. Trump also added during the second presidential debate, "Obamacare is a disaster. You know it. We all know it. It's going up at numbers that nobody's ever seen worldwide. Nobody's ever seen numbers like this for health care."

Trump claimed that it was excessively costly for people as well as for the nation.

He explained, "It's going to be one of the biggest line items very shortly. We have to repeal it and replace it with something absolutely much less expensive and something that works, where your plan can actually be tailored. We have to get rid of the lines around the state, artificial lines, where we stop insurance companies from coming in and competing because they want and President Obama and whoever was working on it, they want to leave those lines, because that gives the insurance companies essentially monopolies. We want competition!"

Other Positions

GUN CONTROL

Growing firearm control has been a political non-starter for a considerable length of time. The 1994 restriction on assault weapons lapsed in 2004. In recent years, many states have extended gun rights, and also the rundown of places where guns are permitted. Mass shootings regularly incite gun-control advocates to request that Congress grow regulations, most recently after 49 individuals were slaughtered at an Orlando, Florida club this year. However, those efforts are yet to obtain results.

Extending gun rights has been one of Donald Trump's most constant messages. The Republican candidate calls for upholding gun laws as of and for a rigorous pursuance of violent criminals. Trump's firearm policies likewise call for extending treatment programs for those with psychological problems.

Mr. Trump resists growing the system used to check the backgrounds of gun buyers to include all the deals at gun shows. He calls bans on firearms and magazines "a total failure." On his site, he says: "Law-abiding people should be allowed to own the firearm of their choice." He additionally pushes for a national right to carry that would consider concealed carry licenses from each state. The National Rifle Association has supported Trump on his stance.

Clinton calls for comprehensive background checks that would require all weapon buyers, including all clients at firearm shows, to be cleared through the National Instant Criminal Background Check System. Current law applies to buy through government authorized merchants and does exclude deals by private people. She bolsters changing the law that permits a weapon deal to continue if the FBI has been notable within three business days to find proof to deny that deal. She criticizes the three-day constrain for permitting Dylann Roof to buy the firearm he is associated with using in the 2015 mass shooting at the Emanuel AME Church in Charleston, S.C.

Mrs. Clinton likewise says the laws ought to be adapted to keep firearms out of the hands of domestic abusers, and she is for putting a limitation on what she describes as military-style weapons. She has been supported by a variety of gun-control promotion groups, including the Brady Campaign to Prevent Gun Violence.

GAY AND TRANSGENDER RIGHTS

Trump and Clinton lie on different pages of many gay and transgender rights issues. Clinton is for marriage rights for same-sex couples, Trump, on the other hand, contradicts this position. She argues a North Carolina law, seen by transgender individuals and others as biased that require everybody to use the public restroom equal to the sex recorded on their birth certificate. Mr. Trump approves the existing law. Be that as it may, while Clinton has attempted to highlight her perspectives on gay and transgender rights, Trump hardly says his.

Trump contradicts the Supreme Court choice allowing a national right to same-sex marriage. However, Trump doesn't display his worries about same-sex marriage with the same intensity and passion as that of its adversaries. Asked on Fox News in January if he would select judges to overrule the court decision, he replied, "I would strongly consider that, yes." After a terror attack at a gay night club in Florida, Trump took on the role as a protector of gay and transgender rights, saying he would keep conceivably dangerous Muslim immigrants out of the US.

At first, the business mogul said he was against the North Carolina law on open bathrooms and said that Caitlyn Jenner, a reality star transgender, would be welcome to choose any lavatory of her choice at Trump Tower. Mr. Trump later said he upheld the state's choice to pass the law.

The former first lady turned secretary of state Clinton restricted gay marriage until 2013, favoring common unions. She said her perspectives grew. Before changing her position on same-sex marriage, Clinton had bolstered equal rights on different matters. As secretary of state, she conveyed a speech in 2011 proclaiming that "gay rights are human rights."

Clinton supported the Obama government on its direction in allowing public school students to utilize the bathroom depending on their personal sexual orientation. She supports legislation banning discrimination on the premise of sexual orientation or gender identity in business, housing, public accommodations and different regions. The video declaring her nomination included a gay couple, and her presidential battle has effectively sought gay and lesbian voters.

GENERAL ELECTIONS

Chapter 4

WIKILEAKS

WikiLeaks has released thousands of emails that were hacked from Hillary Clinton's campaign chairman John Podesta as well as other sources.

The first revelation that the WikiLeaks brought to light was that Hillary Clinton has a very close and cozy relationship with the United States main stream media. Donna Brazile, a high level Democate, working for CNN gave Mrs. Clinton's campaign question for upcoming presidential debates.

The WikiLeaks cesspool of John Podesta's emails has uncovered the corruption and deference of Clinton's battle campaign and even her time in office. Issues and revelations came on a daily basis and to such extent that her team had difficulty in keeping track of each one. So here are the top 10 misleading, deceitful discoveries uncovered thus far.

1. Mrs. Clinton had sheltered and odd relationship with the people in media.

> Donna Brazile, a CNN contributor and then consultant to the Democratic Nation Committee gave the Clinton campaign team advanced copy of the CNN town lobby question

that she thought would give Clinton some time. Mrs. Clinton's campaign praised a New York Times columnist for "teeing up" stories for them, and ABC's George Stephanopoulos for pounding home their ideas. The Boston Globe helped Mrs. Clinton's group augment her essence in New England amid the primaries and CNBC's John Harwood gloated to them about hounding Donald Trump during a Republican debate he moderated.

2. The State Department paid special regard on the "Friends of Bill."

After the massive 2010 Haiti earthquake, a senior aide to then-Secretary of State Clinton repeatedly gave special attention to those identified by the abbreviations "FOB" (Friends of Bill) or "WJC VIPs" (William Jefferson Clinton VIPs), referring to the former president. The emails show Mrs. Clinton's State Department prioritized and benefited Mr. Clinton's friends in the $10 billion recovery effort. The State Department also polled the popularity of Mr. Clinton in Haiti and shared the results with him.

3. Mrs. Clinton fought for "a hemispheric common market with open trade and open borders."

> Mrs. Clinton's vision for America to be like the European Union. She reportedly informed investors in a paid speech last 2013 to Brazilian Banco Itau: "My dream is a hemispheric common market, with open trade and open borders, sometime in the future with energy that's as green and sustainable as we can get it, powering growth and opportunity for every person in the hemisphere." Without borders, there are no countries, including the United States.

4. The Clinton campaign was talking with the Department of Justice officials regarding the release of her emails.

> Brian Fallon, Mrs. Clinton's representative, and previous Justice Department staff member seemed to have conversations with sources inside the DOJ about progressing open records claims to ask for access to her messages while filling in as secretary of state. In an email from May 2015, Mr. Fallon said that "DOJ folks" had "informed" him about the up and coming status meeting in one of the claim.

5. The Clinton camp was given information on the release of the Benghazi emails.

> In April 2015, Clinton crusade Deputy Communications Director Kristina Schake alluded to a "tip" from a source with respect to when the State Department intended to discharge Mrs. Clinton's Benghazi messages. Mrs. Clinton's legal counselor Heather Samuelson followed up on the tip, expressing: "Latest: Still aiming for Friday, but potential it gets delayed until early next week because still moving through interagency review process. Will check back tomorrow and keep you posted. Quick update on this — DOS says the release of the 300 will likely happen on Thurs or Friday. Will keep you posted as I hear anything further on my end. Thx."

6. Mrs. Clinton admitted that sometimes her public and private positions vary.

> In a speech made in 2013 in front of the National Multi-Housing Council, Mrs. Clinton pointed out that her public positions may vary with her private positions, since legislative issues is a monstrous business.

> Politics is like sausage being made," Mrs. Clinton said. "It is unsavory, and it always has been that way, but we usually end up where we

need to be. But if everybody's watching, you know, all of the backroom discussions and the deals, you know, then people get a little nervous, to say the least. So, you need both a public and a private position."

7. Mrs. Clinton's representative taunted Catholics and evangelicals as "severely backwards."

Hacked emails demonstrate Mrs. Clinton's campaign representative Jennifer Palmieri and other Clinton associates straightforwardly discussing Catholics being "severely backwards" and imposing that they don't understand "what the hell they're talking about." The April 2011 dialog between Ms. Palmieri and John Halpin, of the liberal Center for American Progress, taunts media magnate Rupert Murdoch for bringing his kids up in the Catholic Church and said that most "powerful elements" in the conservative movement are Catholics.

8. Mrs. Clinton acknowledged she experienced difficulties relating to the battles of the middle class.

In a 2014 speech for Goldman Sachs and BlackRock, Mrs. Clinton revealed her wealth and open persona way of life segregated her from the money related struggles of the vast majority of the nation, saying her recollections of her youth is the way she associates now to regular Americans. "Obviously, I'm kind of far removed because the life I've lived and the economic, you know, fortunes that my husband and I now enjoy," Mrs. Clinton said of identifying with the working class.

9. Mrs. Clinton campaign utilized Benghazi as a diversion from the email scandal.

Mrs. Clinton's campaign attempted to make her email scandal fade amid the Benghazi inquiry by attempting to conflate and confound the two separate occurrences. Mr. Podesta advised assistants in March 2015 to direct the media's concentration from the email outrage to the House Benghazi examination, which they felt had just been painted in the media as a Republican witch chase.

10. The Clinton group strategized on the best way to postpone discharging emails, knowing it was illegal.

In the wake of accepting a subpoena for her emails, Clinton insider Phillipe Reines in March 2015 talked about tactics to use as a reason not to discharge every last bit of her email. It seemed to constitute a cognizant effort of the Clinton camp to baffle and defer a congressional subpoena. Mr. Reines said of the emails: "Not flippantly, and maybe just from Nick's [Merrill, Clinton spokesman] mouth — but rather than going around on how to release the 55k let's just be for what's happening and use this as an excuse. Because we can say even if State has equities, not providing them would put her in legal jeopardy OR we can say happy for them to have it, happy for them to have them as soon as State is comfortable."

TRUMP'S $900 MILLION LOSS

Donald Trump's federal tax returns from 1995, were illegally disclosed by the media. Trump's taxes reportedly showing that he held a $916 million loss, as published by the New York Times, which said it obtained three pages of Trump's tax history documents that year. The documents supposedly came in by mail with a New York City postmark on.

Apparently, the loss was from three of Trump's asset which is his New York, New Jersey and Connecticut state tax filings that were dated way back in 1995. The document showed a $915,729,293 in total losses.

The New York Times paper said the authenticity of the documents was verified by Jack Mitnick, a lawyer and certified public accountant who managed Trump's tax obligations until 1996 and who was believed to be Trump's tax adviser as prepared in one of Trump's New Jersey tax form.

Trump's camp replied to the Times story by issuing a statement that did not affirm or deny the legality of the documents that the New York Times posted, saying "The only news here is that the more than 20-year-old alleged tax document was illegally obtained." The statement also writes, "Mr. Trump has paid hundreds of millions of dollars in property taxes, sales and excise taxes, real estate taxes, city taxes, state taxes, employee taxes and federal taxes."

TRUMP TAPE WITH BILLY BUSH

Bush in a statement said he was "embarrassed and ashamed." However, Trump consistently denied having groped women.

Bush, who had remained at "Today" for two months, is the nephew of Republican former President George H.W. Bush.

Bush, a father of three, said in the note declaring his leaving and that he was "deeply grateful for the conversations I've had with my daughters, and for all of the support from family, friends, and colleagues. I look forward to what lies ahead."

In the 2005 recording, which was first reported by The Washington Post, Trump discusses fruitlessly seeking a relationship with another "Access Hollywood" employee, Nancy O'Dell.

In the 2005 tape, which was initially uncovered by The Washington Post, Trump talks about unsuccessfully looking for an affair with a certain Nancy O'Dell an "Access Hollywood" employee.

We've pulled some of the lines from Trump from the tape saying "I moved on her and I failed. I'll admit it. I did try and f*** her. She was married," he also mentioned "I've gotta use some Tic Tacs, just in case I start kissing her. You know I'm automatically attracted to beautiful" The then newly married Trump added "I just start kissing them. It's like a magnet. Just kiss. I don't even wait."

However one of the most disturbing and what stuck to most people was Trump saying "And when you're a star, they let you do it. You can do anything. Grab them by the p*ssy, you can do anything."

The two men talked about an actress who was waiting at the end of their bus ride. When they got off, Bush pushed the woman to hug Trump and said, "how about a little hug for the Bushy?"

After the issue on the tape recording got out of hand NBC was quick to decide in firing "Today" show host Billy Bush. The network has initially issued a suspension two days after the tape was reported on October 8.

NBC issued a statement saying "Billy Bush will be leaving the TODAY show's 9 a.m. hour, effective today." The note also said "While he was a new member of the TODAY team, he was a valued colleague and longtime member of the broader NBC family. We wish him success as he goes forward."

Billy Bush's lawyers had since been arranging terms

of his exit before the announcement. The settlement with NBC did exclude a non-contend statement, which means Bush "is a free agent," his legal advisor, Marshall Grossman told the Associated Press. Financial terms of the arrangement were kept classified.

During the second presidential deliberation, Trump said that he never did any of the activities heard on the tape, saying "this was locker room banter, a private conversation that took place many years ago. Bill Clinton has said far worse to me on the golf course — not even close. I apologize if anyone was offended."

Melania, Trump's new wife was quick to help out her husband on the issue, and during a CNN interview she said "I wonder if they even knew the mic was on," Melania added that it was just "boy talk, and he was led on — like egged on — from the host to say dirty and bad stuff."

Regardless of Trump's statement, different women have since accused the business tycoon and said that they had an encounter with him in the past by grabbing or peculiarly kissing them on the lips. However after Trump was elected president all these accusers decided to take no action. Many of the accusers were also found to be lying. Did Hillary pay these women to come forward? Why did not one of them take any kind of action against

Trump with the first 100 days of Trump being elected.

REPUBLICANS NOT SUPPORTING TRUMP

The Republican Party conveyed a remarkable and a surprising ignore to their particular presidential candidate Donald Trump as the Bush family and Speaker of the House of Representatives Paul Ryan, declined to support him.

Paul Ryan, the 54th and current Speaker of the House of Representatives, said he was "not ready" to support Mr Trump, also stating that the time had come to "set aside bullying and belittlement".

This was during Trump's attempt to find a vice-presidential running mate, finding himself rejected after his three initial choices.

Adding up to the list is 2012 Republican Presidential nominee, Mitt Romney. Romney declared that he would not attend the party's scheduled July convention.

The developments pointed the degree of the division and spite immersing the Republicans, and the overwhelming errand Mr. Trump faces to bring together the party.

Hillary Clinton, which at that time stands as a plausible Democratic nominee, tried to underwrite by releasing TV commercial which demonstrated

Trump being denounced by fellow Republicans. The advertisement featured Jeb Bush stating that Mr. Trump "needs therapy" and Marco Rubio referring to him as "the most vulgar person ever to aspire to the presidency."

Trump tried to get back at Jeb Bush during the nomination process suggesting that Jeb has "low energy" and is considered to be an "embarrassment to his family". Jeb Bush's father, former President George H W Bush, had eagerly supported the Republican nominee in each of the five races since he went out, however, his representative said he would not do as such this time. Also, Freddy Ford, a representative for previous President George W Bush, said he "does not plan to participate in or comment on the presidential campaign".

The Rolling Stones also pressed in against Mr. Trump, trying to prevent him from using their music at political assemblies. The British rock band, of which Mr. Trump is a fan, said they had "requested that he cease all use immediately".

Colin Powell, the 65th United States Secretary of State reportedly told the Long Island Association that he is rooting for the Presidential Democratic Party nominee Hillary Clinton.

In spite of the fact that he Powell is considered to be a long-standing Republican, his choice to embrace a Democrat is not surprising. He likewise sponsored Barack Obama in both 2008 and 2012. Nor is it shocking that he would contradict Trump. A comprehensive number of officers, particularly those in the anti-extremist establishment, have reprimanded Trump as favorable to Russia, a nation which is considered to be partially sensitive to the significance of America's key partners, in addition to many other things.

POLLS SHOWING A LESS POPULAR CLINTON AND TRUMP

Donald Trump and Hillary Clinton are considered to be the two most unpopular presidential candidates in more than 30 years of surveys and polling; this is according to ABC News/Washington polls. Studies show that among U.S. adult voters, Clinton has a 59% negative rating, statistically tied with Trump who has a 60% negative rating.

In another survey done by ABC News/Washington Post, 57 percent said they had an adverse feeling of Clinton and Trump. The remaining 46 percent stated they do not have an amicable feeling for Clinton's candidacy and 45 percent have the same to say about Trump.

Of course, we've never had two candidates like this, about whom so many voters had already made up their minds — undoubtedly. It'll be fascinating to perceive how it plays out. Voters see this campaign, as a decision between the lesser of two shades of evils.

Many Americans who detest Clinton say she is not credible. This remained to be one of the eminent concerns behind her candidacy. One-third of Americans claimed she is corrupt. On top of that, the remaining third half said her positions change depending on which the wind blows, which appears a culmination of her integrity. Following these bases, some of her critics even accused the secretary of state as an "unfit" candidate for the presidency and added that she doesn't know enough about the issues.

Trump, on the other hand, faces a different set of challenges among voters.

While Trump, an extremely rich New Yorker, doesn't need to dig the ground to hurt Clinton's candidacy, his issues are also very visible. A fourth of his adversaries said racism is his greatest imperfection. Considering that there are Hispanic and Black-American voters that live in the United States. The percentage of people who would not vote for him reflected a huge 40 percent of Black voters and 35 percent of the Hispanic voters. Another 20 percent claimed that Trump does not have the right experience and background for politics more so the presidency.

This campaign is a battle and a choice between the lesser two evils. Although, it is obviously during the surveys that a variety of voters had undoubtedly decided. The battle remained to be an entertaining and interesting show to watch.

TRUMP'S CARD AGAINST BILL CLINTON

It was clear that Donald Trump was on the defensive, following the two days of conflict and rejection of Trump by many Republicans over a 2005 tape of him and Billy Bush talking about how women in very poor light.

Only an hour and a half before the second Presidential Debate between Trump and Clinton, the businessman turned politician held a surprise live broadcast on Facebook with the ladies who have accused Bill Clinton of sexual assault and in some cases the women accused Hillary of covering it up and turning a blind eye to what had happened.

The women include Juanita Broaddrick, Paula Jones, Kathleen Willey and Kathy Shelton. After Trump addresses his comments on the leaked tape he introduced the ladies and said: "These four very courageous women have asked to be here, and it was our honor to help them."

One of the accusers, Broaddrick previously signed an affidavit stating that Bill Clinton did not rape her, but later retracted her affidavit. Broaddrick said "Actions speak louder than words," she went on and added "Mr. Trump may have said some bad words, but Bill Clinton raped me and Hillary Clinton threatened me. I don't think there's anything worse."

The surprise forum and the frill of the particular subject are remarkable on the eve of a debate, primarily for a presidential campaign.

During the second presidential debate, the then debate host and CNN news anchor Anderson Cooper professed a question directed toward the Republican nominee Donald Trump on the released 2005 Access Hollywood video that found him saying that he felt entitled to "grab them by the pussy." "For the record, you're stating you never did that?" the news anchor pushed. Trump, making light of his comments as "locker room talk," denied he had ever kissed or grabbed ladies without permission. "No one has more respect for women than I do." Trump added.

His dissent, however, has invited women who are currently accusing him to press charges and complaints. These women blame the real estate mogul for indecent behavior from grabbing on planes to undesirable approaches in the Trump Tower.

The presidential hopeful has firmly denied the attribution. His campaign team in a desperate move and warn lawsuits against those media outlets who distributed unverified claims.

First, a secret recording captured Donald Trump that he groped and kissed women without their consent. At that point, came reports that on The

Howard Stern Show in 2005, Trump himself told the host that he walked into dressing rooms while pageant contestants were exposed. Presently more than twelve ladies have approached, both distinctly and secretly, to attest to the fact that Trump did precisely that.

Some of Trump's accusers were driven to speak out after hearing Trump's statement that he had not grabbed women without their permission. Motivated by the recording between Trump and Bush, concerning Trump gloating about grabbing and kissing women.

Listed below are some of the names of the accusers and their brief encounter with Trump.

Ivana Trump, Trump's ex-wife
In spite of the fact that she now says her story was "without legitimacy," in a separation statement in 1992, Ivana Trump depicted a vicious sexual assault by her then-husband.

Kristin Anderson, former model
Trump came to up her skirt at a dance club without having been introduced to her and touched her vagina through her clothing, she said.

Temple Taggart, Pageant contestant - Miss Utah 1997

The shocked 21-year-old Miss Utah title holder was shocked when the business mogul introduced himself by kissing her on the lips.

Mariah Billado, Pageant contestant - Miss Vermont Teen USA 1997
Billado claimed that while they were naked and about to change Trump suddenly barged into their dressing room. Billado and a few other contestants ages 15 to 19 were present during this incident.
Karena Virginia, Yoga instructor
Virginia alleged Trump of grabbing her by the arm and touching her breast back in 1998 US open when she was waiting for a car service outside the venue.

Tasha Dixon, Pageant contestant - Miss Arizona 2001
Dixon has the same claims with Mariah Billado. Dixon who was 18 at the time of the 2001 pageant, stated that Trump "just came strolling right on in," when the contestants were changing into bikinis.

Natasha Stoynoff, former People magazine reporter.
Stoynoff was assigned to cover Trump during the early 2000s. Stoynoff claimed that during the time that she was working on a news feature on Trump. The businessman pushed her against the wall and sexually assaulted her and said: "We're going to

have an affair."

Jessica Leeds, Businesswoman
She had a chance to sit with Trump during a flight, who she claimed grabbed her breasts and tried to reach up her skirt.

Lisa Boyne, Health food entrepreneur
At a dinner, Trump looked up women's skirts and commented on their underwear and genitalia.

Jill Harth, makeup artist
Harth got the chance to met with Trump during a business deal and alleged Trump of repeatedly kissing and groping her.

Summer Zervos, The Apprentice contestant
Zervos claimed that when she visited Trump in his New York office, the real estate mogul kissed her on the lips. Invited her for supper, but rather took her to a hotel, grabbed her and attempted to engage in sexual relations with her.

Some of these women have had stories that have not checked out, while others claimed they have told people at the time when the alleged event occurred. But none have brought forward any direct proof that any of these events occurred. However, that does not mean that the alleged incident did not occur, it just means that by law a person is deemed innocent until proven guilty in front of a court.

Did these women came forward wanting to ride the publicity of the Trump and Bush tape? Were they offered some kind of financial support by the Clinton Campaign, or were they just trying to help the Hillary campaign.

The fact is we don't know why these women came forward, but we do know that based on the information that we have gathered from other witnesses, they are stating that most of Trump's accusers are not telling the truth about the incident.

A strong testament to this is, not one of these women has brought any legal case against Trump. Even after the first 100 days of his presidency.

TRUMP AND CLINTON PERCEPTION BY PEOPLE

From the begin of the campaign period, people were skeptical on who to choose between Clinton or Trump because people believe that it will be a battle between two leaders neither of which they want to be president.

On a survey done using registered voters as correspondents, only 27% of them said that Trump would make a good president. 15% say he would be an average.

Perspectives of a potential Hillary Clinton administration are just to some degree less negative. Around three-in-ten (31%) say she would be an awesome or great president, contrasted and 22% who say she would be normal and 12% who think she would make a poor president. While 33% of the correspondents say Clinton would be terrible as a president.

Supporters of Trump and Clinton are confident that their bet would perform an excellent job as a president. A 68%-in general of Trump supporters says that he would make a great (23%) or good (45%) president. This is very similar what Clinton got in terms of positive views.

Of course both Democrats and Republicans are

included in these polls. So what we can conclude is that both candidates are either loved or hated by people based on these limited polls.

Clinton not telling the truth

People do not want to trust Hillary Clinton because of the email server scandal, Wikileaks because Clinton has stated that she had multiple positions on the issues because of her past. However, most people that don't trust her can describe her in one word, "liar."

According to a Washington Post-ABC News poll done in March 2016, 37% of Americans said that they trust Clinton. Three months later, another survey done by Rasmussen found that 46% of the people surveyed said that Clinton was less honest compared to other politicians

This couldn't be more suitable to a government official like Clinton, who is infamous because of her private email server controversies not to mention being caught numerous times for delivering misleading statements and telling half truths and lies. And now more than ever, with left and right evidence, Hillary Clinton's political career has been painted by deceit.

Hillary Lied about Classified information being sent to her private unsanctioned email server. James

Comey the director of the FBI testified that there was classified email sent to Hillary's server at a congressional hearing. Comey called Hillary "extremely careless"

"I'm not making excuses," Clinton said at a rally in Ohio. "I've said it was a mistake and I regret it," said Clinton in one of her rallies.

Clinton insisted that "what I did was allowed." She maintained that she "opted for convenience to use my personal email account, which was allowed by the State Department, because I thought it would be easier to carry just one device for my work and for my personal emails instead of two." However these statements are not true. The government does not allow classified material to be stored on unsecure systems. Hillary's system was unsecure.

A political consultant insisted that the more Clinton "can do to change the subject so her conversations are around the topics" and matters her campaign is concerned with, the better. This is apparently the best move that the Democratic nominee can do to shift attention away from all the controversies surrounding her.

Trump calling women degrading names

Republican presidential candidate Donald Trump says he can't particularly remember offending women, however, there are always two sides of a story. According to some of Trump's accusers Trump had a history of mainly relating women to animals.

Here are some of the instances on which Donald Trump has allegedly displayed lack of class and has shamed women.

Back in 2012, the business mogul aimed at the co-founder and editor-in-chief of the Huffington Post, Arianna Huffington, mocking her divorce and teasing her appearance. Trump tweeted "is unattractive both inside and out. I fully understand why her former husband left her for a man—he made a good decision," referring to Huffington. Again in 2015 Trump issued a tweet saying "How much money is the extremely unattractive (both inside and out) Arianna Huffington paying her poor ex-hubby for the use of his name?"

On Celebrity Apprentice: All-Stars which aired last 2013, he fantasized on the picture of former Playboy Playmate Brande Roderick stating "It must be a pretty picture. You dropping to your knee."

He called opposing counsel in a deposition

"disgusting" for wanting to break to pump milk for her 3-month-old daughter.

In 2011 Trump attended court to testify when the complainant's lawyer Elizabeth Beck requested for a recess to breastfeed her three-month-old baby. Trump's council objected, Beck then pulled out her breast pump in hopes of proving her appeal. Trump later walked out the court room calling the Beck "disgusting".

His daughter Ivanka, is not an exception on this list. In an interview back in 2006, he joked on national television that if it weren't for a fact that Ivanka was his daughter, he would be dating her. Before that, in a 2004 radio interview, Trump told Howard Stern that he didn't mind if the host refer to Ivanka as "a piece of a**"

Also in the year 2006, Trump was caught in a quarrel with Rosie O'Donnell. The fight grew and countless shots were fired from both camp. Trump in an interview said "Rosie O'Donnell is disgusting, both inside and out. If you take a look at her, she's a slob. How does she even get on television? If I were running The View, I'd fire Rosie. I'd look her right in that fat, ugly face of hers and say, 'Rosie, you're fired!" He added "We're all a little chubby but Rosie's just worse than most of us. But it's not the chubbiness - Rosie is a very unattractive person, both inside and out."

In Trump's book, How to Get Rich, the business tycoon wrote: "All of the women on The Apprentice flirted with me—consciously or unconsciously. That's to be expected."

Even the biggest of all celebrities is on the list. When Angelina Jolie had a falling out with her father Jon Voight, Trump was ask to give a statement on CNN's Larry King. Trump went on saying "I really understand beauty. And I will tell you, she's not - I do own Miss Universe. I do own Miss USA. I mean I own a lot of different things. I do understand beauty, and she's not."

Trump has lost the support of leading Republicans. A number of Republicans has already called that the 70-year-old businessman drops out from the race.

Trump refuse to drop out of the race and issued a statement apologizing for his conduct. Later when pressed by multiple people to drop out of the presidential race and let Hillary win, Trump indicated that he would get back on track issuing a statement saying "I'd never withdraw. I've never withdrawn in my life. No, I'm not quitting this race. I have tremendous support."

TRUMP RALLIES VS CLINTON RALLIES

During the 2016 presidential campaign, we saw Republican nominee Donald Trump gather a huge crowd on his speeches in convention centers, parks, and even airport hangars. However, Hillary Clinton's rallies were small and even at times with only a few hundred people. Sources said that she and her campaign team apparently struggled to be able to fill small colleges and community centers. The news media would not cover this, and almost never showed the empty halls where Hillary campaigned.

It seemed as if the only way Clinton was able to get any kind of crowd would be when she brought in some other star to help her out. Political names like First Lady Michelle Obama, Senator Bernie Sanders and even the President himself Barack Obama were there to show their support. Towards the end of the campaign, the former first lady even invited big celebrity names like Jay-Z, Pharrell Williams, and Katy Perry. It was evident that Clinton's campaign team did the best they could but fell short in making a significant impact at Clinton's rallies.

In Tempe, Arizona, a place that is not a popular campaign stop compared to Florida, Wisconsin, New Hampshire and Pennsylvania; Clinton was able to pack more than 10,000 people in attendance. A political analyst explained that this was expected in Arizona as the people from this state are not hounded by campaign rallies.

Trump was quick to notice the difference between his rally and Clinton's. He bragged "I have to say, we have rallies like this and we have seven, eight, nine, ten thousand routinely," in the North Carolina rally. He also added "Hillary goes out for rallies and yesterday I think she had 200 people, maybe 300."

Lara Brown, a George Washington University professor of political management, tells us that size does not always equal substance. She explains that "Trump has also regularly been going to places where he is most beloved, not where the ground game is most competitive." She also added that "Trump is a novelty and for some, to say that they went, is like saying they went to a sporting event." Lara Brown was previously aligned with the Democrats, but later said she was more of a moderate. Perhaps a moderate Democrat. In any case, the analysis of the ground game turned out to be wrong. Trump understood the electoral college and was able to win the election.

It is a fact that Trump held quite many more rallies than Democratic nominee Clinton. To be exact, Trump's hard work yielded him 53 more events compared to the Clinton camp. Also, math tells us that on an average Trump gets more than 6,000 people on his rallies versus Clinton who only averages about less than 1,000. That is a significant difference that may have allowed Trump to carry more of the swing states.

CLINTON 9/11 COLLAPSE

Hillary Clinton collapses, either passed out or lost control of her body, this is evident in a video clip, as she prematurely leaves from the 2016 9/11 celebration. Clinton's specialist said the scene was an aftereffect of heat and dehydration.

Clinton was seen being aided by her security detail after she fell as she was making her way to her vehicle. A news channel caught up with some witnesses and one, in particular, describes the Democratic nominee as "clearly having some type of medical episode."

Sources that spoke off the record stated that Clinton might have seizures when exposed to the sun. Other sources have indicated that Hillary has Parkinson's disease.

After over an hour of news blackout, Clinton's team released a report saying that the former First Lady "felt overheated," two days later they issued a formal statement blaming pneumonia and lack of hydration as the primary reason for the collapse

Prior the incident, Clinton was believed to have a chronic case of allergies that resulted in her having coughing fits. Clinton's physician, Dr. Lisa Bardack said in the statement. "On Friday, during follow-up evaluation of her prolonged cough, she was diagnosed with pneumonia. She was put on antibiotics and advised to rest and modify her schedule. While at this morning's event, she became overheated and dehydrated. I have just examined her and she is now re-hydrated and recovering nicely."

People accused Clinton of being awfully quiet about her health condition. This lead to the Democratic nominee's decision to release her medical records supporting her claim of good health.

Following the Clinton medical records issue, Trump also asserted on releasing his health records. A confident Trump said, "Last week I took a physical and when the numbers come in I'll be releasing very, very specific numbers." And when the businessman was asked about Clinton's health, he has this to say' "I think it's an issue."

When WikiLeaks released thousands of email, the cozy and inappropriate relationship between the main stream media and Hillary Clinton was exposed. John Podesta, Clinton's campaign chairman, had his email hacked. Thousands of these emails were released to the public by WikiLeaks. These emails shed light as to why the members of the press and the Democratic party nominee share a comfortable relationship.

Apparently, there were email exchanges to and from Clinton's campaign chairman John Podesta. Among the shocking revelations contained in the exchanges includes an advance copy of debate questions and the guarantee of positive coverage in favor of the Democratic nominee: Hillary Clinton.

The Democratic campaign team officials have not disavowed the validity of the emails, but rather have tried to point the finger at Russia for providing the hacked correspondence to the WikiLeaks group, and have cautioned that they could be doctored. However, to date, no series challenge with any kind of evidence concerning the validity of any of the WikiLeaks emails has occurred. Even after the first 100 days of Trump being president, there has been no evidence that the Russian's were the ones that hacked the email account of John Podesta. It could have someone from within the democratic party, or it could have been a high school hacker that guessed that the password for John Podesta's Gmail account which was 'password'. It is laughable that someone would have a password which is 'password'. This is something a kid who watches Big Bird on Sesame Street could hack. It would not take a minor super power like Russia to hack this account. The report that this is Russia could very well be fake news put out by the main stream media as just another way to support Hillary and the Democrat party. The Media has a real credibility issue here and there is no evidence that has been put forward that shows the Russians are to blame.

Donna Brazile, a former CNN contributor and Democratic party insider that has been the acting leader of the Democratic National Committee, messaged members of the Clinton campaign when she worked at CNN to tip them off about a question that would be asked at Clinton Bernie Sanders' debate, her strongest opponent for the Democratic primary.

Brazile sent advance notice to the Clinton camp with detail about a question concerning lead poisoning which was a question that was asked in a debate on March 6th, 2016. Later on Marth 12th Brazile passed on another question concerning the death penalty. Brazile initial denied that she gave any questions, but later came clean and admitted that she had given questions to the Clinton camp.

In another hacked email released by WikiLeaks, a staff member at The Boston Globe had all the earmarks of being contriving with Clinton's crusade to boost her so-called "presence" amid her primary race against Sanders. In the email from Marjorie Pritchard, the Globe's opinion piece supervisor, Podesta inquired as to whether the Clinton campaign was still set to present a commentary. Pritchard went ahead to offer direction on how the campaign could get an advantage by synchronizing with the Globe's standard reporting. Pritchard wrote in the email "It would be good to get it in on Tuesday, when she is in New Hampshire." And the latter part read "That would give her a big presence on Tuesday with the piece and on Wednesday with the news story. Please let me know."

Christina Reynolds, Clinton's assistant, was congratulated in a 2008 email for "single-handedly" persuading a Washington Post columnist to push a story about Cindy McCain, Arizona Sen John McCain's better half. "This is truly outstanding! Great work!" as noted by Paul Begala from the Democratic party.

The Trump campaign team issued a statement saying "We feel disappointed," Conway said. "It is disappointing to read those emails." Also, pointing out that the disclosures of secret communications between individuals from the press and the Clinton team threaten the probability of free and fair elections. The press in the United States is given special protection, however when those protections are abused, and media try to help one political party secretly while trying to pretend that they are neutral is very dangerous. Such practices, should they continue, could lead to the media being highly regulated, and monitored by the government. This is exactly what a free nation does not want.

FBI PROBE INTO CLINTON FOUNDATION

After having been sworn as the Secretary of State During Obama's first term as President, Clinton gave her word and signed a document with the Obama administration to distance herself from the Clinton Foundation. In the agreement, Hillary agreed, that the foundation would limit incoming foreign aid and donations.

Without a doubt, several of the foundation's top donors were Foreign governments or foreign officials. The Obama administration was concern about conflict of interest between Hillary's position as Secretary of State and Hillary's role with the Clinton Foundation. However, the Obama administration could not have been that concerned since they did nothing to stop her activities.

There is an array of evidence to confirm that both Clinton and the foundation neglected to keep their word. The emails that were discovered by the FBI suggested that Clinton held her position in the foundation while holding office as the Secretary of State. The FBI had gathered proof that Clinton had allowed access and favored donors in exchange for aids to the Clinton Foundation.

Basically what happened was the following. Somebody wanted or needed the Federal government to do something, Hillary would send Bill Clinton to give a speech for $500,000 that would be put into the foundation. Then magically what the foreign official or person needed would get done by the State Department which Hillary headed. This, of course, would be illegal for anyone to do, because it would mean that one was using their government position to enrich themselves.

Apparently, the Clinton Foundation received millions of donations from foreign governments while Hillary was Secretary of State department.

The story got its limelight because of a book was written by Peter Schweizer entitled "Clinton Cash" that allegedly uncovers pressing issues of the State Department involving big favors given to top donors of the Clinton Foundation.

An FBI investigation revealed that more than half of Clinton's private visitors during her term as the Secretary of State were donors of the Clinton Foundation. They also discovered a number of emails that suggest that donors received special access and consideration from Clinton and her office.

COLLUSION BETWEEN WHITE HOUSE, JUSTICE DEPT, MEDIA AND CLINTON CAMPAIGN

Democratic officials of the Clinton Campaign had ongoing discussions with officials within the justice department. A WikiLeaks email from Clinton Campaign spokesman Brian Fallon said "DOJ folks" had informed him about a court hearing regarding Hillary's private email server. Republicans said that this shows a collusion between the DOJ and the Clinton Campaign. Emails retrieved through the freedom of information act show that the Obama white house was colluding with the Hillary Campaign in March of 2015. In one email from the white house communication director to the State Department. A request to cancel media appearances of John Kerry, the new secretary of state so that any questions about scandals could be avoided. In another email conversation, the state department told Hilary Clinton's legal team that they did not reveal Hilary's use of a private email server to the Congress.

The Republican National Committee additionally summoned the questionable airplane tarmac meeting between Attorney General Loretta Lynch and Bill Clinton. This meeting took place while a criminal investigation of Hillary Clinton was also taking place. It is entirely inappropriate for the

Attorney General to meet with the husband of the person that is being investigated for criminal activity.

Reince Priebus, who was acting as the RNC Chairman, in a statement, said "Emails showing the Department of Justice was giving Hillary Clinton's campaign inside information about an ongoing investigation into her email server is deeply disturbing and raises, even more, questions about Bill Clinton's tarmac meeting with Attorney General Loretta Lynch."

ELECTIONS OUTCOME

Chapter 5

ELECTION EXPECTATIONS

The United States election is the electoral college system where each state that is won by a candidate provides them with a certain number of delegates. To win the presidency, a candidate must collect 270 delegates. A week before the election the survey appears there are still just enough swing states to allow for a Republican to win the presidency.

For the Republicans to win they needed to dominate in states like Pennsylvania, Michigan or Virginia, where most polling data showed the Democratic nominee leading.

Many thought it was impossible, but to some political analysts, this scenario was conceivable, and it could be supported by polling that underestimates white voter turnout or overestimates Mrs. Clinton's support in key voting demographics like blacks and the young.

For this plan to work, Trump should basically be impeccable or polling would need to be off in a mixture of distinct states that have clearly diverse voters. A mistake in New Hampshire surveying, for example, wouldn't mean calculations in Florida would probably be wrong. A miss in Michigan would have a small bearing on the outcome of Colorado.

TRUMP vs. CLINTON

Polls recommend that if European countries were to choose Hillary Clinton, she would unanimously win. Governments across the region are giving careful consideration and evaluating how they will function with the succeeding administration, especially if it will be led by Donald Trump.

The New York businessman-politician has discovered a few allies among a huge portion of Europe's community, both in transient vigilant Eastern Europe and in Western Europe, where against immigrant, anti- EU supporters in Germany, France, and Britain are trusting a Republican triumph will support their causes.

Trump's opinion on the sensitive subjects of migration and job are being shared by only a few people in the European nation, but, it charms him to devotees of grassroots movements over the region who see their countries as losing their authority and their business under what some see as a European super state.

According to the European foundation, their concern is about the new American leadership's ability to stay connected with Europe, therefore they are putting their bet in favor for Clinton.

German Chancellor Angela Merkel has this to say about Clinton "I admire her strategic thinking and her strong commitment to the trans-Atlantic partnership."

The Chancellor's sentiment matches that of numerous Europeans who consider Clinton to be sharing needs that are trademarks of European traditional liberalism.

A day before the election, Clinton has managed to maintain her edge in the polls. In a race between a Democrat, a Republican, and 2 third-party nominees, Clinton retains an average lead of 3.2% over Trump.

Based on the FiveThirtyEight website, which regularly updates their data, spots a 31.5% chance of winning for Trump compared to the former 30.9% possibility that Trump got.

Towards the election day, Clinton campaign team choose to be careful yet confident. For them, Trump winning the Presidential position would need to be viewed as an unassuming shocked.

Trump's manager Kellyanne Conway and transition team leader Chris Christie were at the New York Hilton Midtown to pre-celebrate with the Republican supporters as the night of vote tallying went on. The venue was packed with the Republican nominee's supporters. Among present was known Celebrity supporter Stephen Baldwin, the crowd looked like they were already celebrating even before the initial results went in. As more results went in, it already became evident that a Republican nominee had bagged the position as the President.

Not far away was Clinton's campaign team who choose to gather at Javits Center. As the night of tallying went on the Clinton supporters grew anxiously, and then the tense feeling quickly turned into a heartbreak as it became evident that the party no longer on the running for the Presidential position. It came to a point that Podesta, the Democratic campaign chairman came out and convince the crowd to rest and head home, leaving them a promise that Clinton will appear days later to deliver her speech.

Many were surprised as a more detailed tally was released, showing that the Democratic candidate lost where she believes she had the advantage.

These states include Pennsylvania, Michigan, and Wisconsin. As John Podestra said: "They're still counting votes and every vote should count. Several states are too close to call, so we're not gonna have anything more to say tonight," as he was trying to comfort the supports. But a few minutes following this statement Trump received a call from Clinton, to express that she had conceded. According to sources, Clinton was urged by the Obama saying in a phone conversation "You need to concede." The Obama call was controversial as claimed by some Clinton supporters who believed that the Secretary of State should have waited a few more hours for the official announcement.

However, Clinton was keen on acknowledging her loss and said: "I'm calling him," then again insisted saying "Just give me the phone."

The Green Party head Jill Stein, pushed for a recount and Clinton's camp was having second thoughts on joining Stein. Apparently, Clinton's camp and the White House does not share the same sentiments with regards to the recount. However, days following the event the Clinton campaign team supported the Green Party and proposed to launch a recount particularly on the ballots for states of Michigan, Wisconsin, and Pennsylvania.

The then presumptive President Trump had condemned the efforts for a recount stating: "Hilary

Clinton conceded the election when she called me just prior to the victory speech and after the results were in." He also insisted on saying "Nothing will change."

ELECTION RESULTS WHICH STATES WENT FOR WHO

After millions of Americans have gone to the polls and voted we can now decide on a winner.

Once the votes had been tallied, it turned out to be apparent that surveys amid the campaign had failed to predict the situation.

Hillary Clinton's pre-election day lead faded away as Donald Trump cleared the board to topple the Democratic nominee. Essential states including Florida, Ohio, North Carolina and Pennsylvania filled for the disputable Republican.

It was a crushing loss for Clinton, who did not go to her campaign HQ following the results.

Trump Wins

Texas	(38 Electoral Votes)
Florida	(29 Electoral Votes)
Pennsylvania	(20 Electoral Votes)
Ohio	(18 Electoral votes)
Georgia	(16 Electoral Votes)
North Carolina	(15 Electoral votes)
Indiana	(11 Electoral Votes)
Tennessee	(11 Electoral Votes)
Missouri	(10 Electoral Votes)
Wisconsin	(10 Electoral Votes)

TRUMP vs. CLINTON

Alabama	(9 Electoral Votes)
Colorado	(9 Electoral Votes)
South Carolina	(9 Electoral Votes)
Kentucky	(8 Electoral Votes)
Louisiana	(8 Electoral Votes)
Oklahoma	(7 Electoral Votes)
Mississippi	(6 Electoral Votes)
Arkansas	(6 Electoral votes)
Kansas	(6 Electoral Votes)
Utah	(6 Electoral Votes)
Iowa	(6 Electoral Votes)
West Virginia	(5 Electoral Votes)
Nebraska	(5 Electoral Votes)
Idaho	(4 Electoral Votes)
Montana	(3 Electoral Votes)
North Dakota	(3 Electoral Votes)
South Dakota	(3 Electoral Votes)
Wyoming	(3 Electoral Votes)

Clinton Wins

California	(55 Electoral Votes)
New York	(29 Electoral Votes)
Illinois	(20 Electoral Votes)
New Jersey	(14 Electoral Votes)
Virginia	(13 Electoral Votes)
Washington	(12 Electoral Votes)
Massachusetts	(11 Electoral Votes)
Maryland	(10 Electoral Votes)
Colorado	(9 Electoral Votes)
Oregon	(7 Electoral Votes)
Connecticut	(7 Electoral Votes)

Nevada	(6 Electoral Votes)
New Mexico	(5 Electoral Votes)
Hawaii	(4 Electoral Votes)
Rhode Island	(4 Electoral Votes)
Maine	(4 Electoral Votes)
Vermont	(3 Electoral Votes)
Delaware	(3 Electoral Votes)
DC	(3 Electoral Votes)

RIOTS IN STREETS

A number of people were not pleased with the election results, thousands of militants rally to the streets of New York Manhattan as they march towards the Trump Tower. People in thousands choose to gather at Manhattan park to show their dismay on Trump's victory as they shouted: "Not my president!"

According to the police report, an estimated 6,000 demonstrators were present and they were able to block traffic in Oakland, California. Militants burned trash in the middle of an intersection, a small group lit up fireworks, while other destroy storefront businesses. As some of the protesters hurled objects at the police, the police were forced to react by tossing chemical irritants, as told by witnesses.

In downtown Chicago, 1,800 gathered outside the Trump International Hotel and Tower while chanting phrases like: "No Trump! No KKK! No racist USA!"

The Chicago police closed roads in the area, as thousands gathered outside Tump International Hotel and Tower. However, there were no records found or immediate reports of an arrests or violence.

In Los Angeles, protesters sat on the 101 Hollywood Freeway, blocking traffic as police in riot gear watched. A 22-year-old protester was seen carrying a placard saying "Enjoy your rights while you can." The particular rally was joined by mostly high school and college students that are reported to have reached 5,000 in number.

Demonstrators also gathered in Seattle. There were initial reports of a shooting that allegedly had casualties, near the venue where the anti-Trump rally was held. However, police said that upon further investigation the shooting was not related to the rally being held that night.

Hundreds of America's youth also took part of the rally. Concerned young high school and college students walked out in protest in Seattle, Phoenix, Los Angeles and Oakland, Richmond and El Cerrito, California.

Protesters were furious about Trump's program that they considered being racist, along with the plan to build a wall at the Mexico border, to keep out undocumented immigrants.

Hundreds likewise rallied in Philadelphia and Boston. In Austin Texas, there were around 400 individuals who walked through the streets, as accounted by a police officer. The media were seeking for a reaction from the Republican camp but the Trump campaign was not keen on giving away any statements during the hype of the protest.

A Latino crowd of around 300 high school students stepped out of their classes in Los Angeles to show their support for the anti-Trump campaign. They were shouting "El pueblo unido nunca será derrotado" which in English means 'the people united will never be defeated', they were also seen carrying signs such as "Not Supporting Racism, Not My President" and "Immigrants Make America Great" printed on them as they walked towards the City Hall. The students held a wild yet brief rally.

Many of those students were members of the "Dreamers" generation, children whose parents entered the US with them unlawfully, school officials said, and who fear deportation under a Trump administration.

In his victory speech, Trump insisted that he would be a president for all Americans, saying: "It is time for us to come together as one united people." The Republican team also said, "Mr. Trump and his campaign denounces hate in any form".

MAX VANGUARD

EXPECTATION OF WHAT WILL FOLLOW

Chapter 6

TRUMP SUPREME COURT JUDGES

President-elect Donald Trump is that peculiar president who will likely assign a Supreme Court justice subsequently to taking office. He is expected to have a huge role in shaping the composition of the Supreme Court for the coming decades.

Following the death of Justice Antonin Scalia, who died in February, then President Obama called for Merrick Garland to replace Scalia's seat. However, the Senate Republicans refused to hold a hearing for Garland. This means handing the decision to incoming President Trump to fill at least one seat on the country's highest court.

During an interview with Sean Hannity, Trump stated he has narrowed down his original list of 21 people to "probably three or four." Trump said on Fox News Channel "They are terrific people, highly respected, brilliant people. We'll be announcing that pretty soon."

Among those who are also expected to leave the justice court and retire is 78-year-old Stephen Breyer and 83-year-old Ruth Bader Ginsburg.

The Republican candidate has shown bolster for exceptionally conservative judges. He said he needs to topple Roe v. Wade, the point of interest case giving women the privilege to abortion, and stated that the Court needs to "uphold the Second Amendment."

Trump's rundown of candidates contains some surprising selections, for example, Utah Sen. Mike Lee. Generally, majority of Trump's potential candidates have a background in supporting conservative issues.

To date here are Donald Trump's potential Supreme Court nominees:

1. Keith Blackwell
2. Charles Canady
3. Steven Colloton
4. Allison Eid
5. Neil Gorsuch
6. Raymond Gruender
7. Thomas Hardiman
8. Raymond Kethledge
9. Joan Larsen
10. Mike Lee
11. Thomas Lee
12. Edward Mansfield
13. Federico Moreno
14. William Pryor
15. Margaret A. Ryan
16. Amul Thapar
17. Timothy Tymkovich
18. David Stras

19. Diane Sykes
20. Don Willett
21. Robert Young

REPLACE OBAMACARE

Congress returns to work a week after the election, and one of the priority is to look inside and strip Obamacare.

In order to replace the existing Obamacare, legislation would require 60 votes in the Senate, however, the Republicans do not have the strength in numbers to counter the Democrats seated in office.

Rather, Republican officials rely upon the gut key arrangements of the law utilizing the budget reconciliation process. This procedure is constrained to arrangements that influence government incomes and spending and requires just a simple majority to pass. It would empower Congress to remove the Obamacare. Additionally, it can get rid of the government subsidies, wipe out funding for Medicaid expansion and eliminate a significant number of Obamacare-related expenses.

Donald Trump's victory over Hillary Clinton predicts well for the future of America's healthcare system.

With Obamacare in an all out "downward spiral," voters were plainly in no condition for Clinton's proposal to "expand on" the president's health care law. Rather, they picked a president who has said that his first request of business will be to "ask Congress to quickly convey a full nullification of Obamacare."

According to President Obama and his partners, it's an open question. As he hands it over to the Clinton campaign rally days before the election, Obama stated that the Republicans "got no plan" to replace Obamacare.

However, under Speaker Paul Ryan's direction, House Republicans have put forth an alternate plan, and according to Ryan he described it as "A Better Way." He continued and maintained that the house is working on a more detailed health care plan compared to that of what Obama has off his sleeves. Ryan said that the system would run on an expanded coverage that guarantees to reduce expenses and also preserve those with existing health conditions.

Ryan said that as of the moment everything is still on paper. The next round is to work on an official legislation and then proceed with the federal cost estimates. Once executed, it promises to strengthen in places where Obamacare did not.

BUILDING A WALL ON MEXICAN BORDER

Donald Trump has always been put in hot water because of his policy regarding illegal immigrants and his illustrious talk on building a wall along the US-Mexico border.

The newly appointed Republican presidential Donald Trump ended his soft approach on immigration policies, during the campaign last September 2016 he said that he would deport undocumented immigrants living in the US and renewing his claim of having Mexico pay for the wall that he was planning to build along the border. Aiming at the citizenship for immigrants who were already in the U.S., Trump said: "There will be no amnesty!" "Mexico will pay for the wall 100%." Trump added, "They don't know it yet, but they're going to pay for the wall". To which the crowd responded shouting, "Build that wall!"

Trump claims the wall is necessary since the Mexico border is a gateway for illegal immigrants, criminals, and rapists' to come to the US.

But will the construction be underway soon? Will the Republican businessman follow through on this bold campaign promise?

The Mexican border wall was one of Mr. Trump's most eye-catching and outlandish policies.

According to the Department of Government at Exeter University's Dr. Gina Yannitell Reinhardt, it is "unlikely but not impossible" that Trump will be able to build the wall.

However, Dr. Reinhardt was quick to weigh in and said, "He needs a lot of money to do that. Congress does not support building the wall. It would be a very complicated endeavor."

Mexico has already made it clear that they will not fund the building of the wall. Nonetheless, Mexico asserted that they would keep their good relations with the US and will work with President-elect Trump for the benefit of both nations, but repeated that they would not pay for his planned border wall. Mexican President Peña Nieto even met with Mr. Trump in September and stated: "I made it clear that Mexico will not pay for the wall."

There are slim chances of Trump winning his battle with Congress as he seeks approval and funding for the construction project. Chances are that the Congress could block the plan in the Senate and House of Representatives.

Based on record there is already an existing 650 miles long wall out of the 2,000 miles long border, however, there were still reports that drug cartels constantly tunnel under it.

Trump has estimated the wall to cost roughly around $12 billion but fact shows that it could easily equal to double of Trump's calculation.

Spanish newspaper La Vanguardia said it is "unlikely" that we will see the construction of a wall between Mexico and the United States. The newspaper said, "In spite of the immense amount of money that the project would cost, its construction could give him grave problems with his Latin American neighbors and the rest of the world."

And even acknowledge that "it is not clear that Congress would support this initiative."

TRADE DEALS – RENEGOTIATE

Trade is one of the key issues during the election. And since America has now chosen a new President, United States is expected to experience a few changes on trade policies. It was reported that Trump had accused China and Mexico over stripping job opportunities from the US, in return the Republican candidate wants to impose high tariffs towards both countries.

The new administration is yet to announce their plan on trade, but based on Trump's statement towards China, we can somehow already see what's coming. Analysts say that US could resort to limiting imports of steel and aluminum from China into the U.S. with a goal to get control over a surge of low-quality metal imports that have had a huge impact on U.S. manufacturers.

Also, we can see that Trump will take a step towards strengthening its executive branch focusing on China's currency control. China is regularly attacked for fictitiously increasing the value of Yuan in a way that they can sell goods and services of cheaper value.

These activities would likely mean making an option for nations to settle trade issues, which the World Trade Organization administers. While the WTO principles are exceptionally important, they are two decades old and no longer fits the trend on what trade is today. Having recognized this the government under Trump's leadership is assumed to summon the president's unilateral trade authority as an influence on deciding some issues through proper negotiation.

The Trans-Atlantic Trade and Investment Partnership between the US and the European Union is likely on the backend of Trump's trade priorities. After United Kingdom had decided to leave EU, negotiations went slow and uncertain. Granting Trump's judgment towards free trade, it is likely that they will re-evaluate the existing trade agreements and the chances are that they are going to opt for an extended break before the Trump Administration chooses to hold a discussion on the so-called partnership.

But the Republican party has made it clear that they do not want to throw away the current trade agreement but insisted on making better agreements. However, they have not disclosed any information on which agreement applies to which country. Being that UK and US share the same sets of standards in terms of our products and services, UK would be a perfect choice to set-off renegotiations on trade agreements

To add to the list of renegotiation is NAFTA or the North American Free Trade Agreement. Trump still can't seem to explicitly indicate what's the downside of the agreement other than that it had a huge effect on U.S. employment. Currently, the new Administration is yet to decide on what steps to take, but sources say that they have already made efforts to set renegotiation talks.

According to the Constitution as President, the 70-year old businessman-politician has jurisdiction over the agreements, he can approve or forgo the agreement without Congress, this could only mean that the Countries involve will have no choice but to represent themselves at the negotiating table.

According to the Constitution as President, the 70-year old businessman-politician has jurisdiction over the agreements, he can approve or forgo the agreement without Congress, this could only mean that the Countries involve will have no choice but to represent themselves at the negotiating table.

MAX VANGUARD

REFERENCES

TRUMP vs. CLINTON

URL LINKS

http://www.foxnews.com/politics/2016/11/02/fbis-clinton-foundation-investigation-now-very-high-priority-sources-say.html

http://www.politico.com/magazine/story/2016/07/hillary-clinton-emails-history-214095

http://www.people-press.org/2016/08/18/clinton-trump-supporters-have-starkly-different-views-of-a-changing-nation/

https://www.nytimes.com/2016/10/02/us/politics/donald-trump-taxes.html

http://www.denverpost.com/2015/08/25/colorado-republicans-cancel-presidential-vote-at-2016-caucus/

http://www.newsday.com/opinion/oped/colorado-super-tuesday-rules-disenfranchise-most-voters-1.11525395

http://edition.cnn.com/2015/09/01/opinions/sexton-trump-carson-fiorina-outsiders/

http://www.ranker.com/list/2016-presidential-candidates-controversies/ranker-news

http://2016.republican-candidates.org/

http://2016.democratic-candidates.org/

http://www.news.com.au/finance/work/leaders/do-super-delegates-rig-the-democratic-primaries-in-hillary-clintons-favour/news-story/590348429e8eb7fcbee22961c2a909aa

https://www.washingtonpost.com/news/post-politics/wp/2016/06/06/in-a-tense-exchange-bernie-sanders-says-his-refusal-to-quit-is-not-sexist/?utm_term=.e1e5e3fbb07b

https://www.hiiraan.com/news4/2016/Sept/117880/clinton_stays_calm_while_trump_loses_cool_during_first_presidential_debate.aspx

http://fortune.com/2016/10/09/heres-who-won-the-second-presidential-debate/

http://learningenglish.voanews.com/a/us-vice-presidential-candidates-debate-policies-of-trump-and-clinton/3538045.html

https://www.forbes.com/sites/vickyvalet/2016/09/25/hillary-clinton-vs-donald-trump-where-the-candidates-stand-on-employment-and-jobs/#66aa9b835e55

http://www.wsj.com/graphics/elections/2016/donald-trump-hillary-clinton-on-social-issues/

http://www.aljazeera.com/programmes/listeningpost/2016/10/wikileaks-political-hacks-election-161023102730794.html

https://www.nytimes.com/2016/10/02/us/politics/donald-trump-taxes.html?_r=0

http://www.foxnews.com/entertainment/2016/10/18/nbc-news-fires-billy-bush-after-lewd-donald-trump-tape-airs.html

http://www.latimes.com/nation/politics/trailguide/la-na-trailguide-updates-reluctant-trump-supporter-paul-ryan-1475907609-htmlstory.html

http://fortune.com/2016/08/21/millenials-dont-like-donald-trump-or-hillary-clinton/

http://www.politico.com/story/2016/10/donald-trump-bill-clinton-accusers-229441

http://www.thedailybeast.com/articles/2016/10/12/all-of-donald-trump-s-accusers-a-timeline-of-every-alleged-grope-and-assault.html

http://www.aljazeera.com/blogs/americas/2016/11/hillary-clinton-donald-trump-rallies-161104233413813.html

http://rightwingnews.com/hillary-clinton-2/hillarys-doctor-releases-diagnosis-video/

http://www.foxnews.com/politics/2016/10/12/bias-alert-wikileaksexposes-medias-secret-support-clinton.html

http://www.foxnews.com/politics/2016/10/11/republicans-claim-collusion-after-email-appears-to-show-doj-clinton-campaign-contact.html

http://www.mirror.co.uk/news/world-news/who-winning-election-2016-results-922177

http://www.businessinsider.com/president-elect-donald-trump-supreme-court-list

http://www.express.co.uk/news/politics/730583/Donald-Trump-will-US-President-build-wall-border-Mexico-America-Mexican-illegal-immigrants

https://en.wikipedia.org/wiki/United_States_presidential_election,_2016

https://en.wikipedia.org/wiki/Results_of_the_Democratic_Party_presidential_primaries,_2016

http://www.justfacts.com/globalwarming.asp

http://www.cnn.com/2016/07/05/politics/fbi-director-doesnt-recommend-charges-against-hillary-clinton/

http://www.cnbc.com/2016/07/07/rep-trey-gowdy-rips-into-fbi-director-james-comey-on-hillary-clintons-intent.html

http://www.epi.org/blog/naftas-impact-workers/

https://www.scientificamerican.com/article/sun-spots-and-climate-change/

http://www.cnsnews.com/news/article/susan-jones/clinton-explains-why-she-said-one-thing-chelsea-something-else-benghazi

https://www.thenewamerican.com/usnews/crime/item/23532-benghazi-probe-obama-officials-refused-to-address-gun-running

http://www.nationalreview.com/article/430153/fast-furious-obama-first-scandal

http://www.kiplinger.com/article/taxes/T056-C000-S001-where-clinton-and-trump-stand-on-taxes.html

http://www.washingtontimes.com/news/2016/oct/12/top-10-hillary-clinton-scandals-exposed-wikileaks/

http://www.politifact.com/punditfact/statements/2017/jan/06/jesse-watters/claim-john-podestas-email-password-was-password-la/

http://dailycaller.com/2017/03/15/justice-department-sued-for-records-about-lynchs-tarmac-meeting-with-clinton/

www.ingramcontent.com/pod-product-compliance
Lightning Source LLC
Chambersburg PA
CBHW072123280526
45788CB00002B/523